*Praise for I Should Be Burnt Out By Now…
So How Come I'm Not?*

"This book is a timely reminder of just how much we can do to control our own lives and ensure our own mental well-being. It's a practical guide filled with wide-ranging examples of how people have taken charge of their own lives in trying circumstances to not only avoid burning out, but to thrive. An uplifting read for anyone with a hectic and stressful life, which is, let's face it, all of us."

*— Neil Bradford
Managing Director
Forrester North America*

"Understanding burnout and how it happens is imperative in this day and age. The bottom line is, burnout is a choice. You can keep it from consuming you, and this book shows you how."

*— Jeffrey J. Jernigan
President & CEO
Union Bank*

"Here is the how-to guide on thriving in today's highly competitive world. The authors take their own advice and 'lean into' the lives of many people, drawing conclusions and checklists that inspire reflection and action in order to live a happy, fulfilling life. This is a book you'll want to keep going back to."

*— Janice Wismer
Vice President, Human Resources
Canadian Tire Corporation Ltd.*

I SHOULD BE BURNT OUT BY NOW...

So How Come I'm Not?

I SHOULD BE BURNT OUT BY NOW...

So How Come I'm Not?

HOW YOU CAN
SURVIVE AND THRIVE
IN TODAY'S UNCERTAIN WORLD

PEG NEUHAUSER · RAY BENDER · KIRK STROMBERG

WILEY

John Wiley & Sons Canada, Ltd.

National Library of Canada Cataloguing in Publication

Neuhauser, Peg, 1950-
    I should be burnt out by now... so how come I'm not? : how you can survive and thrive in today's uncertain world / Peg C. Neuhauser.

Includes index.
ISBN 0-470-83385-8

    1. Success in business. I. Title.

HF5386.N48 2004   650.1   C2003-906701-7

Production Credits
Cover and interior design: Interrobang Graphic Design Inc.
Printer: Tri-Graphic Printing

Printed in Canada
10 9 8 7 6 5 4 3 2 1

Contents

Acknowledgements   xiii

Chapter 1: Introduction   1

Not Burning Out…One of Your Best Skills   2

What Does Success Look Like?   3

So What's the Secret of their Success?   4

The Structure of This Book   4

Five Key Messages on Avoiding Burning Out   5

Part One: Mindset and Attitudes   7

Chapter 2: Watch Your Thoughts   9

What Kinds of Thoughts Protect You?   12

The Anatomy of Optimism   13

The Power of the Present   16

Focus on the Present to Get You through Really
Tough Times   16

When You Do Think about the Future, Paint a
Positive Picture   20

Mental Toughness and Discipline Keep You from
Burning Out   21

Contents

Chapter 3: Find the Meaning   **25**

Finding the Passion—Have a Heart   26

Finding the Purpose—Make a Difference   28

Finding the Commitment—Be a Part of
Something Bigger Than You   30

Living with Courage and Conviction   32

Chapter 4: Get a Grip on What Really Matters   **35**

Making the Tough Choices   37

Don't Sweat the Petty Stuff, and Don't Pet the
Sweaty Stuff   40

Stick to Your Standards   41

Keep Your Eye on the Prize   43

Chapter 5: Keep Your Options Open   **45**

Ask Yourself What You Don't Want   46

A Four-Step Process for Building Your Options   47

Step One: Develop a Vision for Your Life   47

Step Two: Conduct Continuous
Environmental Scanning   49

External Scanning   50

Internal Scanning   51

Step Three: Build a Portfolio of Options   53

Step Four: Be Prepared to Change   55

Checklist for Keeping Your Options Open   57

Chapter 6: Be Careful How You Tell Your Own Story   **59**

What's Your Story?   60

Are You a Hero or a Victim in Your Story?   61

Is the Tone of Your Story Funny or Tragic?   63

What's the Moral of Your Story?   64

Have You Created a Superhero Reputation
for Yourself?   65

Part Two: Habits and Actions 69

Chapter 7: Laugh More Than You Whine 71
    Laugh at Things That Aren't Funny 72
    Use Humor to Connect with People and Make a Point 74
    Allow Yourself Self-Pity Breaks 75
    Use Humor to Keep Things in Perspective 77
    Use Laughter to Blow Off Steam 78
    Laughter Brings People Together 79
    Smiling Works as Well as Laughing 81

Chapter 8: If You're a Control Freak, Get Over It 83
    If You Don't Trust Them, You Can't Delegate to Them 84
    Inspect What You Expect 85
    Don't Take Over When the Team Gets Bogged Down 87
    Being Overly Helpful Is a Control Freak in Disguise 89
    You Can't Always Save the World 91

Chapter 9: Develop Healthy Rituals 93
    Use a Variety of Healthy Rituals to Rejuvenate 93
    Not Your Typical Healthy Rituals 94
    Getting Enough Sleep 97
    Breathing Is a Healthy Ritual 98
    Taking Time Off 99
    Pacing Yourself Is an Essential Daily Ritual 100
    The Trap We Can All Fall into If We Aren't Careful 102
    Checklist of Your Healthy Rituals 103

Chapter 10: Get Organized 105
    If Getting Organized Doesn't Mean Cleaning
        Off Your Desk, What Does It Mean? 107
    Self-knowledge: The Key to Coping with Complexity 108
    Relationships with Others: When Everyone Wants
        a Piece of You 110

Time: The Common Enemy 112
  Whose Monkey Is This? 113
  Too Many Irons in the Fire 114
Technology: Taming the Beast 114
  The Palm Pilot vs. the Spiral-Ring Notebook 115
  Find Somewhere to "Dump" Your Ideas 116

Part Three: Connections and Relationships 119

Chapter 11: Build a Network of Strong Relationships 121
Value of Friends at Work 121
Downside of Friends at Work 122
Loyalties Keep People Going through the
  Rough Times 125
Using People You Trust as Resources 126
How Large Is Your Network of Connections? 129
Be a Good Friend 131

Chapter 12: Defending Yourself from Toxic People 133
First Choice: Eliminate Toxic People 134
Second Choice: Limit Your Contact 135
Third Choice: Confront the Toxic Person 137
Surround Yourself with People Who Give Back 138
Are You a Toxic Person? 140
Toxic Person Checklist 142

Chapter 13: Be a Good Team Member 143
Three Traits of Effective Team Members and Leaders 144
Make the Boss and the Organization Look Good 144
Cooperate and Share the Credit 146
Get Along with Everyone 148
Helping the Team Survive Discouraging Times 151

Part Four: Organizational Setting—Is It Helping or Hurting You?   **153**

Chapter 14: Is Your Work Culture Burning You Out?   **155**

What Is a Work Culture?   156

Is There a Mismatch between You and Your Work Culture?   157

Are You Working in an Abusive or Unproductive Culture?   159

What Is a Healthy Work Culture?   161

Pay Attention to Culture When You Apply for a Job   163

Checklist One: Hallmarks of an Inspiring Culture   165

Checklist Two: Indicators of a Toxic Culture   166

Chapter 15: Are You Being "Held Captive" by Your Organization?   **169**

Three Types of Captivity   170

Financial Traps   170

Structural Traps   172

People Traps   175

You Can't Keep Doing Things the Same Way   177

"Held Captive" Checklist   178

Chapter 16: Are You Working for a Toxic Boss or an Inspiring Leader?   **179**

Toxic Bosses vs. Inspiring Leaders   180

How Much Do You Trust Them?   181

Toxic Bosses Believe in Theory X   181

Toxic Bosses Inspire Career Changes   182

Inspiring Leaders Energize Their Followers   184

Learning to Lead   187

Toxic Boss Checklist   189
Leader Checklist: What Do We Want from Leaders?   189

Chapter 17: Conclusion   **191**
Anti-Burnout Checklist   192

Bibliography   **199**

Index   **201**

Acknowledgements

The people that we interviewed created this book. Even though the three of us did the actual writing, we simply followed their lead recounting the stories and advice they gave us. We would like to thank all of these people for taking the time to be interviewed and allowing us to quote them extensively throughout the book. Without their wisdom and sense of humor, this book would not have been possible.

Each of us have personal role models who have been the inspiration for writing this book, but Ray wanted to make a special acknowledgement of Art Redfern. Art overcame war, business setbacks, personal loss, and cancer but keeps on ticking.

This has been our second opportunity to work with the team at John Wiley and Sons Canada led by our editor, Karen Milner. Both experiences have been as close to flawless as life ever gets. It has been a classic example of great teamwork in action. Thanks to everyone at Wiley for making this book a pleasure to write.

Working behind the scenes, Steve Engler edited and refined our writing before it ever reached Wiley, and Denise Bugg produced a thousand pages of interview transcripts at a rapid-fire pace to keep us on schedule. Thank you to both of them. We would like to offer a special thanks to Linda Goold for her review, advice, and wonderful sense of humor that helped shape this book. She is the fourth member of this writing team and we could not have done it without her. Thanks Kirk, you married well. After Culture.com, Peg claimed she was willing to write a book with this team again anytime. It was a great experience once again.

Introduction

Remember the old Timex watch commercials on television? "Takes a licking and keeps on ticking" was the message. The watches were put through all kinds of dramatic punishments, but in the end those watches were still ticking. The people you will read about in this book are like those watches. Their histories are filled with the usual range of life's hard knocks, setbacks, and heartbreaks, but they found ways to survive and keep on ticking.

A few comments from the interviews:

> During my nine-month job search, I didn't really have any choice about burning out. I'm a very literal person. Failure was not an option. *Ina Lavin, human resources executive who was laid off*

> When I leave one job or task and go to another, I leave it and take on the other one. I don't allow any overlap. I work hard and do my darnedest, but once it's done,

it's done. *Chad Reese, full-time manager, part-time university teacher, and married father of three children under seven years old*

I've always made an effort to have change in my life. Sometimes it was as small as changing the route I drove to work. I've changed jobs an average of once every four years. It helped me experience more, which has benefited my career. I guess that's why losing a job would not be the end of the world to me because I know there are other jobs out there. *Vickie J. Jones, insurance accounting operations manager and single mother of two children with a mother who has Alzheimer's*

I'm incapable of feeling sorry for myself. The first time I saw a small child in the treatment center, all feelings of self-pity disappeared. These children are unbelievable role models of courage and fortitude. I was encouraged by the older people too. They were experiencing great pain, but showed up every day ready for treatment. I was humbled by the way people acted with grace, although they faced an uncertain future. *Joe Galuszka, management consultant, married father of two children, and a cancer survivor*

Not Burning Out . . . One of Your Best Skills

There has been a great deal of talk during the past two decades about the serious problem of stress and burnout. Most of the discussion focuses on the pessimistic side of the story. The underlying assumption is that we are in a fierce struggle, one that we frequently lose. Burnout is presented as almost inevitable, and solutions focusing on recovery are offered.

There is another, more optimistic side to the story. What about the people who endure tough times with courage and grace, or bounce back from crises with renewed energy when logic tells you the situation should have left them depleted and discouraged? For all the talk about burnout, the fact is that the majority of people spend most of their lives coping amazingly well. We are far more resilient and skilled at surviving and thriving than we give ourselves credit for. We take our successes for granted and pay relatively little attention to the skills and strategies used every day to handle whatever life throws at us.

What Does Success Look Like?

The people described in this book are not perfect. None of them claimed superhero status, and they would laugh at the suggestion. They told stories about tough times, failures, and struggles. Many described times in their lives when they burnt out for a while or at least came very close to doing so. But generally over the course of their lives, they functioned fairly well during uncertain or difficult times. Three key elements describe their success—most of the time they were able to:

- cope with disruptive change
- produce high-quality work
- live a happy or satisfying life

When these three things were not happening in their lives, they regained their footing fairly quickly and got back on track.

So What's the Secret of Their Success?

There are thousands of success stories every day about people who continue to survive and make the best of tough times. So how do they do it? What are the real stories of how individuals survive and even thrive during uncertain and difficult times? And what is their advice on preventing burnout?

This book answers these questions. The solutions are in the form of stories and tips from real people. Research for the book was conducted through interviews and surveys with people from a wide variety of occupations, ages, and geographical regions. The stories and tips in this book are taken from 1,000 pages of transcripts from seventy in-depth interviews and the results of 400 surveys.

The Structure of This Book

This book is divided into four parts covering the major themes emphasized in the interviews and surveys.

The figure represents the relationship among the four themes. As you move out from the center of the circle, the topics move from the internal, personal issues to the external, environmental issues.

Five Key Messages on Avoiding Burnout

The following statements are representative of the common messages that came up consistently in the interviews. Although everyone worded their opinions differently, there was a surprising degree of agreement across professions, age, geographical region, and gender.

Don't Wait for the Right Circumstances

You can't sit around waiting for the right circumstances to fall into place so you can be happy. Take the attitude that you will make the best of life no matter what the circumstances. When things get tough, don't wait to be rescued. Rescue yourself.

If You're Not Dead, It Can't Be That Bad

It's all about keeping things in perspective. People get too worked up about things that really don't matter that much. If the situation isn't going to kill you, maybe you are overreacting and wasting your energy.

It's a Skill That Takes Practice

Being good at not burning out is a skill more than a genetic personality trait. Just like any skill, you have to work at it. You can learn to manage your behavior and your thinking, but it takes discipline and practice to do it.

Nobody's Perfect

You can't get it right all the time. But when it all gets to you and you lose it, just get a grip on yourself again as fast as you can and keep going. There is no perfect score on this one. Just keep bouncing back.

Don't Look Back

Don't keep looking back over your shoulder at past mistakes or rough times. Learn everything you can from the experiences, and then let it go and move on. Don't waste your energy on the past.

PART ONE

Mindset and Attitudes

"Is the glass half empty, half full, or, as the engineers say, twice as big as it needs to be?"

"Mindset and Attitudes" is Part One because the people we interviewed told us that's where it belongs. *How* you view your life is much more important than *what* is actually happening to you. These individuals have dealt with some of the hardest blows life can deliver—cancer, business failures, death, and miserable job situations—and survived. In many cases, they did more than survive. These situations were turned into worthwhile experiences from which they learned valuable lessons.

> "I'm not a cancer survivor. I'm a cancer thriver!"
> — *Cheryl Jernigan, community activist and former association executive*

> "I have had major goals that were dashed—absolutely dashed. I prayed myself through those times. If you wallow, you are sunk. After a brief period of necessary mourning, I had to determine what had happened and how to recover."
> — *Ginna Gemmell, president and founder of GlidePath® from Alexandria, VA*

Some people describe themselves as mentally tough. Others say they are resilient and bounce back from adversity. And there are those who talk about drawing strength from their belief in a higher spiritual source. Each person uses different language and concepts and gives a variety of advice, but everyone agreed that mental attitude is key. Get that right and everything else follows.

Watch Your Thoughts

"**B**right people have the capacity of freaking out faster and more dramatically than anyone else."[1] Burnout starts in the brain. Kelsey August, a thirty-four-year-old entrepreneur who has started and led three businesses and was the youngest woman to make the Inc. 500 list, described a scene from her life when her thoughts were getting in her way.

> I remember when I hit my first wall. I was in a business owners' group that met once a month. I got on my high horse at that meeting and started venting. "I'm expected to do everything around there. I have to do this, I have to that…" They let me go on for about twenty minutes and then one of them looked at me and said, "You're the business owner. What do you *think* your job description is, Kelsey? It's no different for anyone else around here, and if it is, it's because their business has matured. But it is impossible not to go through what you are going through for the first five years."

---

[1] David Allen, *Getting Things Done: The Art of Stress-Free Productivity* (New York: Viking, 2001), 240.

Obviously, that was not the response I wanted to hear. I was upset with their answer. I didn't sleep well that night thinking about what they had said to me. And the next morning, I got up with a new perspective. I went into work and said to myself, "This is my job and I'd better start liking it."

Thoughts are not automatic and uncontrollable like your breathing or heartbeat. You can choose your thoughts. Change your thoughts and you can alter your mood, energy level, and probability of success. Staying in a bad mood is almost impossible after shifting your thoughts to something pleasant, interesting, or inspiring. Most people engage in frequent conversations with themselves. This is often referred to as self-talk or "chatter." Pay attention to your conversations in your head. If they are often cynical or self-deprecating, change the conversation to something more positive and constructive. Many people spend entirely too much time thinking about (and talking about) their problems. It is, of course, necessary to spend some time thinking about your problems so you can plan how you will deal with them. But many people go over and over the same ground without any productive outcome for all that thinking. People who are good at avoiding burnout have developed the discipline to manage their thinking. If it didn't come naturally to them, they practised until they were in the habit of choosing their thoughts.

TIP ONE	If you want to improve your mood quickly, change your thoughts. It is impossible to stay in a bad mood if your thoughts are upbeat. Be careful not to spend too much time thinking about (or talking about) your problems.

Barbara Glover and Ray Rasmussen, a couple who both work in the technology industry, described their efforts in this way:

> We believe that everyone has habits, and smart people manage those habits. A positive mental attitude is a habit just as much as the routine of putting your keys in the same place every time when you walk in the house. We do things like come up with our own personal mantras. Every day, morning and night, you say the same thing over again. And you find yourself thinking about it during the day. It is entirely possible to manage the habits of your life, including your thinking.

A number of people we talked to mentioned that they used repetitious phrases (which are often called mantras, affirmations, or prayer) to keep their thoughts on track. The phrase can be anything that captures a positive aspect of who you want to be or how you want to respond to events. Here are some examples:

- I am a successful, happy, healthy person.
- I love my work, and I am going to enjoy it today.
- I will think about today, not tomorrow or yesterday.
- I will sleep soundly and wake up refreshed.
- Thank you for all the gifts in my life.

TIP TWO

Make up phrases that help you develop the mental outlook you want. Repeat them often each day. They will help you develop the mental habits you want.

What Kinds of Thoughts Protect You?

Barbara Glover described how to develop the habit of choosing your thoughts:

> You always have at least ten things you can be thinking about, and you can only really think about two or three at the same time, so pick the two or three things that have a chance of producing a positive outcome. Keep your mind focused on those, and don't think about the others. Why waste your energy on the others?

One common theme from the work of experts specializing in the study of happiness is that the *content* of your thoughts is a key element to being happy. The experts use different language and models to describe the types of thinking that work; the following list of twelve categories reflects most of their suggestions. Think of these categories as guidelines for choosing the topics and tone of your thoughts. (See the Bibliography for books by Seligman, Carlson, or Baker.)

Thoughts That Are Good for You

Gratitude

Love

Optimism

Courage

Humor

Sense of Freedom and Options

Spirituality

Purpose or Meaning

Proactivity

Curiosity

Altruism or Kindness

Health and Energy

These categories—with the exception of the first two items, which topped everyone's list (i.e., the experts and the people we interviewed)—are not in order of importance. Thoughts of gratitude and love on a regular basis are the most powerful in producing more happiness and less burnout. However, all twelve categories are useful in producing calmer, happier, less stressed moods. One person interviewed put it this way: "This sounds corny, but I think sometimes it's a matter of counting your blessings and appreciating what you have, particularly in this day and age. Try to appreciate what's positive about the situation and focus on that." Another person described how she builds gratitude into her daily meditation: "When I do breathing exercises, with each inhale I think of something in my life I am grateful for and with each exhale I say 'thank you.' It's very calming. Even on the worst days, I can always think of dozens of things in my life to appreciate."

TIP THREE

The following twelve categories of thoughts are good for you. Practise the habit of thinking these types of thoughts throughout the day. The two in bold are the most important to practise regularly: **Gratitude, Love,** Optimism, Courage, Humor, Sense of Freedom and Options, Spirituality, Purpose or Meaning, Proactivity, Curiosity, Altruism or Kindness, Health and Energy.

The Anatomy of Optimism

Martin E.P. Seligman, Ph.D., one of the leading authorities in the study of positive psychology, described the mechanics of optimism as having two major components: permanent vs. temporary, and universal vs. specific.[2]

When people form the habit of viewing failures or bad events as temporary and specific to that one situation, they are more optimistic or hopeful. On the other hand, when faced with failure or a bad event, some people have the habit of seeing the situation as permanent and universal. "It will always be that way and will affect everything I do." When faced with adversity, thoughts running in the direction of "always, never, everything is bad" will burn you out more easily. This kind of thinking is often referred to as "catastrophizing." A habit of catastrophizing ensures that tough times will take their maximum toll. The circumstances were the same for the optimist and the pessimist, but their opinions about the situation were very different.

Craig Park, a senior executive in the building industry, talked about a time in his life when the technology company where he was an officer went bankrupt, he was sued by the acquisition company, he was getting divorced, and "just to throw gasoline on the fire, my mother passed away. It was hugely stressful." When asked how he got through it, most of his answers related to how he thought about himself and the situations he was facing.

> Self-confidence and an optimistic outlook. I approach things with the attitude of "What can I do here?" It's not a problem that I can't overcome. And there's a patience piece too. Things happen over time. We all have highs

---

[2] Martin E.P. Seligman, *Authentic Happiness: Using the New Positive Psychology to Realize Your Potential for Lasting Fulfillment* (New York: The Free Press, 2002), 88.

and lows in our lives and our careers. I have a very long view and see these short-term events as only pieces of a much longer story. I'm still writing that story, and this is just a chapter. I might not be able to see the path ahead, but I know in my heart it's there and I will work through it.

One cancer survivor we interviewed told us that her surgeon helped her face her situation with optimism. He phoned her the day the test results came in to tell her she had breast cancer.

> Once he knew I had heard what he was telling me, he went on to be very optimistic. He said it was the smallest tumor he had ever seen a pathologist find. My prognosis was very good. He told me to look at it as a speed bump in my life. Get through the treatment and then get on with my life. I kept saying that over and over to myself as I went through treatment. This is one hell of a speed bump, but then I will get on with my life. And that's exactly what I did.

TIP FOUR

Being optimistic is not magic and does not require a lifetime of good fortune. When you obsess in the "always, never, everything is bad" mode, make yourself stop. Practise shifting your thinking to "this is a temporary, specific problem. I will deal with it and get on with my life. It's just a speed bump in my life."

The Power of the Present

Will Rogers once said, "I know worrying must be effective because almost nothing I worried about ever happened." Life happens entirely in the present. No one has lived a single day in the past or future. The past and future exist only in our minds, and yet much of the misery people impose on themselves comes from their thoughts about the past or future. The events occurring in the present often are more pleasant or neutral than the "events" in your thoughts of the past or future. Even if current events are terrible, your only chance to affect their outcome is to concentrate on what is happening and be prepared to take action.

TIP FIVE	Develop the habit of keeping most of your thoughts focused on the present. Pay attention to the details of your life today. When you obsess about the past or future, pull yourself back to today. Concentrate on (1) what you can do today to steer your life in the right direction and (2) the simple pleasures of events around you. For example, did you actually taste that great cup of coffee you had this morning?

Focus on the Present to Get Yourself through the Really Tough Times

In a number of interviews, people described situations that were very difficult to endure. They often said that the only way they got through these experiences was to rely on the age-old wisdom to "take it one step at a time." They would narrow their focus to the immediate present and not let themselves think about the weeks or months ahead. One interviewee told a story about how he survived a particularly rough time in his life when he was young. What he learned from this experience changed his life.

> I was about twenty-two years old, barely returned from a Mormon mission and assigned to a Mash unit in the National Guard. I knew I needed to transfer out of that unit because we were screwing around all the time and I was going to get court-martialed if I stayed there. One evening we provided medical support on a parachute drop for a Special Forces unit. I was so impressed I asked to be transferred to their unit. They let me do it with the warning that I had to go to parachute school and it started in six weeks.

> We got to Fort Benning for jump school in the heat of the summer. After four days, I felt completely defeated. We had to get up at 3:30 every morning. It was fiendishly hot and humid. The training was really rigorous. I wasn't in very good shape, so every morning I found myself in the Gig Squad. When you couldn't do more than the minimum number of repetitions of certain exercises, they put you in a punishment squad known as the Gig Squad. So all four mornings I had been in training, I was in the Gig Squad. They just wore you out. Every time you made a mistake, they punished you in hopes that you wouldn't make any more mistakes because in the world of parachuting, you can't make any mistakes. You either injure or kill yourself or injure or kill somebody else who is parachuting with you.

So after that fourth day, I announced to the group that I'd had enough and the next morning I was going to drop out. There was dead silence in the barracks. The colonel of our Special Forces unit said, "Why don't you and I take a walk for a minute and you can kind of tell me about it?"

So we walked away from the rest of the group, and he said, "Let me tell you something about you that I've observed. You are very bright. You are very creative. You've got a lot of leadership ability, but it appears to me that you are the kind of guy that every time you run up against some kind of obstacle or have to do something that's a little harder than you anticipate, you sort of bug out of it." And I thought to myself, "Boy, this guy really knows me." Then he said, "I'm going to give you some advice, and then I can tell you what we can do to help you. I don't want you to promise me or anybody or even yourself that you are going to finish this course. I don't want you to promise that you will finish the whole week. I don't even want you to promise that you will get through the next day. But what I'd like you to do is to learn how to make a commitment to yourself that you will get through the next hour. You will find that if you can make a commitment to get through the next hour, you will have success." Then he said, "I'd like you to take a walk by yourself and think about that. Then come back to the barracks and tell us what you really want to do."

I walked around for a while and decided I liked his advice and I decided to continue. When I told the Colonel, he said, "Let me tell you what we are going to do to help you. You're the new guy. The rest of us have all been together, the twelve of us, for a long time. We know each other. We have a lot of loyalty to each other. We haven't included you because you've only been with us for six weeks, so we have all decided that we are going to help you. The way we are going to help you is that somebody is going to be assigned to be with you every hour. Every time that you flag, we are going to give you a little boost." And that's what happened. The training never got any easier. I was in the punishment squad until the last minute, but somebody was dogging me from the unit every minute and saying, "You can do this. Come on. Let's go." So I finished it, and it changed my whole life. It gave me the sense that I could do things I didn't want to do that were unpleasant, hard, and difficult, but I could do them if I could learn that lesson of just doing things one hour at a time and making a commitment to do it. That's the way I have proceeded with the rest of my life.

TIP SIX	When you are facing a really difficult time in your life, sometimes you have to narrow your focus to the immediate present and take things "one hour at a time."

When You Do Think about the Future, Paint a Positive Picture

One of the interviewees recounted how she used positive thoughts about the future to affect her life:

> First, before anything can happen in your life, you have to get a firm view of what that success would look like. Looking back, there was a time when I might have been burning out. I was living in a beautiful apartment and coming home on Friday nights, having a nice bubble bath, a glass of wine, and enjoying music, but I didn't have anybody in my life nor was I trying to meet people. Then I read a book that talked about affirmations, and I started saying to myself regularly that "I have a loving, giving, caring, fun relationship." I would say that as I went to sleep at night. I didn't know what he looked like, but I would picture this relationship. Shortly after that, my friend encouraged me to meet her cousin. She described him as a great guy. We started dating. A few months later I was driving down the highway and it hit me, "This is it. This is the loving, giving, caring, fun relationship I've been looking for."

They have been married for over fourteen years and have two children.

TIP SEVEN | It's okay to think about the future at times. But when you focus on the future, paint yourself a positive picture so the future you're creating is one that you want to live.

Mental Toughness and Discipline Keep You from Burning Out

Mike Suchanick, a COO of an organization working its way through an extremely long and difficult financial setback, talked about how he survived the two years of grueling stress and pressure:

> I've been involved in martial arts for fifteen years. Our instructor, who is a native of Korea, says "Don't waste your energy on things you can't change." I have learned to move quickly beyond the things I can't change, and I attribute some of my ability to do that to the martial arts training. Two phrases we hear regularly in the training are "Never retreat in battle" and "You always finish what you start." I go to class a couple of times a week after work and sometimes I am so tired that I sit in the car and think to myself, "I'm just too tired to go in." I drag myself out of the car and go in to do the class anyway. When I come out an hour and a half later, I always feel better.

Several interviewees attributed at least some of their ability to withstand tough times to rigorous training they had undergone in their lives. A number of these experiences were military: Marine, Ranger, special operations, CIA, and West Point. Ed Gallagher credited Marine training for his mental attitude for facing changes at his company that could leave him without a job. He said he thinks to himself, "Yes, this is terrible and I hate it. It's stressful and I could lose my job, but at the end of the day, I've still got two hands, two arms, and two legs, and I'm alive.

So it's important, but I'll survive. I have other options. And that perspective is helpful to me."

Military or martial arts experience is not the only type of "toughness" training. When one woman interviewed heard about some mottoes that are part of commando training, such as "You don't have to like it, you just have to do it," she laughed and said, "That sounds like my childhood." Mental toughness training can come in many forms. Alice Swearingen, a corporate director, described her history as a college-level competitive swimmer: "You trained six hours a day, 300 days a year, and pushed your mind and body to the limit." When asked what she learned from this experience, she listed the following lessons, which carry through many other life settings:

- Build friendships and value the genuine efforts of other team members.

- Rise to the occasion when you think you have hit your limit.

- Listen to your coach and respect authority.

- Set goals, visualize success, and take pride in your accomplishments.

- Balance your life, make choices, and let some things go.

- Show up mentally and physically every day.

Everyone has gone through "rigorous training" if you view your life experiences this way. Our interviewees described many rugged experiences they lived through (e.g., difficult job situations, illnesses, raising teenagers, going to school while working at the same time, failed businesses or marriages). These experiences can be training experiences that toughen you mentally. Chelsea Shaffer, a mortgage broker, said her stepfather had a saying that she has always remembered: "Lean into it. When it gets rough, you just have to lean into it. Ultimately it's going to go away. You'll get through it."

<table>
<tr><td>TIP EIGHT</td><td>Look at the rough times in your life as "toughness training." You don't have to be a Navy Seal or an athlete to learn lessons from the rugged times in your life. Make a list of what you have learned and apply those lessons to other areas of your life.</td></tr>
</table>

Find the Meaning

Finding meaning in your work is a key factor in avoiding burnout. Almost all the interviewees told us that if their work has meaning, they can tolerate a great deal of chaos. According to some, meaning came from belief in their projects or the organization's goals. Others thought that the process of actually doing work—solving problems, being creative, working with others on teams—created meaning. For many people, finding meaning is a matter of combining their deeply held or spiritual values with what they do every day. For example, if courtesy, loyalty, and honesty are qualities that you prize, regularly practise these qualities at work.

TIP ONE	Look for the meaning in your work. You can tolerate a great deal of chaos if your work has meaning. Incorporate your values in your work life daily.

Finding the Passion—Have a Heart

Passion, no matter how you define it, energizes people. Jack Hawley, management consultant and author, called it "spirit." This is "our aliveness, what is the real us" and "an organization's energy, its vim, vigor and power. We inject energy, release it, expand it and funnel it." Finding that spirit, he said, comes about by "infusing oomph" into the tasks and projects of the workplace.[1] As Harrison Owen, business writer and consultant, noted, "For some people the notion of passion is too wild and uncomfortable ... But anything less just doesn't bring the juices up to a rolling boil. ... Commitment, performance and excellence only emerge when the heart is engaged meaningfully, and that is called passion."[2]

Jim Lunsford, training and recruitment director for Wayne Brothers, Inc. in Davidson, North Carolina, loves what he does. "I wouldn't want the owner to know this, but I'd probably get up and come in here and work for nothing. You don't burn out when you have that attitude. I'm just delighted they pay me for this." Jim talked about the importance of creating jobs that are interesting and inspiring.

> Companies really need to look at work, especially in this era of downsizing. You can downsize to a point that you can overwhelm a person. Or you could create a better job than the person had before. You could make it less boring or give more responsibility. If you are careful to craft the structure of a job, you can make

---

[1] Jack Hawley, *Reawakening the Spirit in Work* (San Francisco: Berrett-Koehler Publishers, Inc., 1993), 37.
[2] Harrison Owen, *Expanding Our Now: The Story of Open Space Technology* (San Francisco: Berrett-Koehler Publishers, Inc., 1997), 27.

it more interesting. There's a guy here who's one of our concrete superintendents. Here's a guy that gets up at three or four in the morning for a concrete pour. He's knee-deep in concrete and absolutely loves to do it. Now I don't understand that, but I admire it.

TIP TWO	Find work that engages your heart and then infuse some spirit into your projects. If you love and enjoy what you're doing, that passion will protect against burnout.

Andy Goodman, a communications consultant for nonprofit organizations and foundations, described passion as "that moment of flow when you're working on a project and two or three hours just disappear. You don't feel the passage of time because you are really into the work and really enjoying it. That's what I experience now." Andy also talked about how people sometimes take their passions and turn them into livelihoods.

People always say, "How am I going to make a living out of making matchstick houses?" But sometimes it's possible. For example, my sister, Jane Pollak, does Ukrainian Easter eggs and has become so good at it that she published a book about it. Her eggs were featured in the White House Easter egg roll. There is one in the Smithsonian. She has been on "The Today Show" with her eggs. That entrepreneurship has now launched her on a career of talking about how to take what you love doing and do it for a living. She wrote a book called *Soul Proprietor*. She speaks on this topic as well. It's just fascinating. She has a talk called "If I can make a living out of this . . ." Making Easter eggs was her passion and that has emerged into a book and a career about turning your passion into a business.

Andy's observations about his sister are consistent with those of Matthew Dunn, chief information officer for Intrawest in Vancouver, British Columbia. Matthew focused on bridging the gap between work and the inner life.

> Have a broad range of interests. It sounds trivial, but it isn't. Intellectually demanding work can drown out other thoughts, considerations, and interests from your brain. We all have only so much attention. But a self-narrowing frame of reference, oddly enough, reduces rather than enhances professional ability. I'd put it more strongly than that. Have *passionate* interests. Meaning shouldn't be solely found in the workplace.

TIP THREE	Cultivate a wide range of interests in your personal and work life. Look for ways to merge your passionate interests and your work. If someone can turn a passion for Easter eggs into a lucrative career, it's possible for you to do the same with your passions.

Finding the Purpose—Make a Difference

John Sebree, a lobbyist for the National Association of Realtors, enjoys his work as a housing advocate and believes it is worthwhile because "I feel like I'm making a difference. I feel like the issues that we lobby are truly good." His colleague, Jamie Gregory, agrees. "I know that the definition of a good lobbyist is that he can be an advocate for any issue. For at least nine out of ten issues I work on, I can be the guy in the white hat. I think that matters. I couldn't work for just anybody."

Not every job is altruistic and not every person is temperamentally disposed to work for altruistic causes. However, that's not the only way to make a difference with your work. The people we talked to uniformly agreed on the importance of feeling some sense of purpose in their work. Alice Swearingen, a director for a global pharmaceutical company, laughed when she commented: "Doing a job that has meaning is so important to me, especially as a working mom. I laugh and joke that if I wanted to be unappreciated, I could stay home and do it in my pajamas. With work, of course I want the compensation, and I also want it to have meaning."

Some of the people we interviewed sought out work where they believed in a principle or a product or an organization. For others, the work found them. Shana Pate Moulton wandered for a while. After college, she worked for a bank and hated it. Then she managed clothing stores and loved it so much that she set a goal of owning a boutique. The boutique took all her energy seven days a week. She realized that working all the time wasn't conducive to having a family, something she eventually wanted. Her mother, aunt, and grandfather had been teachers, so Shana "randomly went back to school. I'll give that a go." She got a teaching certification and then went on for a master's degree and a doctorate. When she started teaching, she "just loved it and felt fulfilled. I was no longer wondering what I should be when I grew up. I just felt like that's where I was doing the most service for other people and for myself."

Nate Gatten, vice president for Government and Industry Relations at Fannie Mae, is a firm believer in having a purpose. "I don't think it can be emphasized too much that you have to have some genuine interest in the cause in which you are engaged." Nate was greatly influenced by a book entitled *Good to Great* by Jim Collins. The book describes great companies that have an "almost cult-like environment." His own company, Fannie Mae, was included in the book. "Fannie Mae is on that list of great companies. It is almost like a cult in the sense that whether you are in government relations or the audit department, or you are one of our bond traders, at the end of the day everyone here has a genuine interest in housing, so we are all very proud of where we work and what we do."

TIP FOUR	Embrace the mission of the organization, no matter if it's based on profit motives or altruistic goals. This is critical to finding meaning.

Finding the Commitment—Be Part of Something Greater Than You

Several people emphasized that being part of something greater than themselves and pursuing it purposefully provided meaning to their work. Here are some of their comments:

> Burnout is the symptom of the deeper problem of not doing what you are meant to do. If you are doing what you are meant to do, burnout never enters the equation. No such thing. *Andy Goodman, communications consultant to nonprofits and foundations*

I'm excited by the thought of being a part of something greater than me. It's a really interesting time to be alive. *Janice Wismer, head of human resources for a large Canadian retailer*

I have never had a job where I haven't found meaning. It is believing you are making a difference and helping someone. *Pat Vinkenes, senior policy maker for the Social Security Administration*

Meaning comes when we become involved in things that are greater than we are as individuals. *Norman La Barge, who worked as a civilian in Vietnam and learned this statement is true even (or especially) in wartime*

You won't be very happy unless your goals include things like making a difference, leaving the world better off than you found it, or getting a challenge and putting something in place. *Jim Lunsford, training and recruitment director for Wayne Brothers, Inc.*

TIP FIVE	Commit yourself to something greater than your own self-interest. Look for ways to make the world better off than you found it. If you're committed to a cause or goal, you're less likely to burn out.

You likely will feel more commitment if you keep learning. Bonnie Barrett, a director at a large pharmaceutical company, said, "When I think of burnout, what I actually associate it with is boredom." One of the people we interviewed worked for Dick Cheney when he was a Congressman. He said he was in a constant state of on-the-job training. "I never got tired of what I was doing. There was always a new challenge. I had to learn everything because I was new to each responsibility. It became a matter of mindset and developing and using the right habits." Amy Turner, human resources representative, typifies the habit of continuing to learn: "I always want to learn more, so I find meaning in what I'm doing, whether it be work or school. This helps me succeed in my career and family."

	Don't lose your curiosity. Keep learning. Commitment comes more easily when you're continuously learning new things. Boredom is a very close cousin of burnout.
TIP SIX	

Living with Courage and Conviction

The three themes of finding meaning through passion, purpose, and commitment are reiterated in a useful book on meaning and spirit. In *The Power of Full Engagement*, Jim Loehr and Tony Schwartz make the assessment that "spiritual energy provides the force for action in all dimensions of our lives, and fuels passion, perseverance and commitment. It is derived from a connection between deeply held values and a purpose beyond our self-interest, and is served by character—the courage and conviction to live by our deepest values."[3]

One interviewee is an entrepreneur who blended all these qualities and, in so doing, found significant meaning for his life. Steve Hill practised law for more than twenty years. When he was in his late forties, Steve worked with a client for several years in an attempt to secure an antitrust verdict against a Goliath of a corporation. Against all odds, they won. The case left Steve very tired (but not burnt out), and the judgment gave him financial freedom to explore entrepreneurial opportunities.

Steve went to a company that was developing ultrafast computers. After he had been there for less than a year, the company was almost out of money. Shortly thereafter, the CEO left, and Steve became acting CEO and president of the company. Eventually a new CEO was appointed, leaving Steve as president of the company. He said that he feels "a lot of loyalty to the new CEO, and from the beginning I have felt like there was a real purpose to this. I wanted to take a small company to a position where it was stable and making a real contribution in our state and local economy. There is some amount of idealism. There is the hope of payoff in the end. Last, there are many aspects that have been a lot of fun." In 2002, Steve's company built the third-fastest supercomputer on earth and the fastest cluster computer system in the world. "The more I've done, the more ambitious I've gotten. I remember when my dad was my age, he was talking about retirement. All I think is 'I'm just fifty-four. There's so much I still want to do.'"

---

[3] Jim Loehr and Tony Schwartz, *The Power of Full Engagement, Managing Energy, Not Time, Is the Key to High Performance and Personal Renewal* (New York: The Free Press, 2003), 110.

Steve's story exemplifies all the dimensions of spirit—passion, purpose, and commitment. His story also contains the character qualities of perseverance, loyalty, and service to his community that helped give his work meaning. Gene Raphaelian, management consultant, provided a recipe for lifelong engagement: "The recipe is simpler than people would imagine. It is this: Find things to do that you love, find people you love to work with, and learn to enjoy what you do and the fruits of what you do."

> **TIP SEVEN**
>
> No matter what your age or stage in life, keep thinking about what you still want to do. Pursue your passions with courage and conviction. The recipe for lifelong engagement is to find things to do that you love, find people you love to work with, and learn to enjoy what you do and its fruits.

Get a Grip on What Really Matters

Keeping things in perspective on what really matters is an essential element of avoiding burnout, according to many people we interviewed. Bob Kulbick, an insurance executive and West Point graduate, told a story from his youth that illustrates the importance of keeping it all in perspective:

> I remember a conversation I had with my Uncle Bert when I was a kid. I was always afraid my parents would lose their jobs and we would be poor. I saw what happened to other kids in the neighborhood. All of a sudden, the family had to move away. We would ask my parents, "Why did they move?" and they told us "Mr. So and So lost his job." So I worried about things like where the money comes from if you lose your job. How are you going to eat? Then one day I was sitting at dinner with my parents and I overheard a conversation that my Uncle Bert lost his job with Firestone, where he had been for twenty-five years. They were talking about how horrible it was, and it was pretty scary. That weekend, my aunt and Uncle Bert came to a family barbeque. I

thought he would be really upset, but there he was drinking beer, laughing, and having fun. I went up to him and said, "Gee, Uncle Bert, you lost your job. Are you worried? What are you going to do?" And he responded, "Bob, in World War Two, I landed on the beach of North Africa. I was transferred just in time to land in Sicily. Then I went to England just in time to land at Normandy. I was the only person in my company that wasn't killed or wounded. After I went through four years of having bullets whizzing by my head and my friends getting killed, I really don't worry too much about losing a job."

Bob thought to himself, "Okay. That puts things in perspective." A few years later Bob entered West Point and had his own experience that cemented the lesson he learned from his Uncle Bert. He described the shock of arriving at the academy.

You come from being a senior in high school, where you are the president of the class, captain of the sports team, top of the class in grades, and an Eagle Scout. But at West Point it's "Yeah, so?" Everybody had that kind of high school background. I have never encountered that level of stress of having so much on the line. Fail one class and you are out. Everything I have done since is a piece of cake compared to those four years.

TIP ONE

Use the difficult experiences in your life to keep a perspective on what matters and what doesn't. If you could survive those tough times, the events you're facing today aren't so overwhelming after all.

Several interviewees participated in an activity developed by Stephen R. Covey and described in his book, *First Things First*. The exercise involved filling a gallon container with rocks, gravel, sand, and water. If you don't put the big rocks in first, you cannot get everything in the container. This exercise reminds people to concentrate on the most important things in their lives. Matthew Dunn, chief information officer for Intrawest in Vancouver, British Columbia, was clear on what is most important to him: "Despite the challenges of the job, it is always my number two priority. My family is always first. Even when the time demands are considerable, I never lose focus on my family as the number one priority. I can't imagine any job or opportunity that would get in the way of that for me."

TIP TWO	Identify the "big rocks" in your life. Once you decide what is most important to you, make sure those things are your highest priority on a daily basis.

Making the Tough Choices

"You can't do everything that needs to be done." This statement was the consensus of our interviewees. Julie Freeman, president of the International Association of Business Communicators, said:

> You do the best you can do and understand that you are a human being. You can't do everything that needs to be done. And the world isn't going to come to an end if you don't make it through your to-do list. You have to give yourself permission to not be perfect. I'm going to do the best I can, but I'm human and I am going to

make mistakes. If you think you have to be excellent at everything you do, then you put a lot of pressure on yourself that isn't healthy.

Many of those interviewed are fairly good at sorting out the "big rocks" from the "little stuff" and using this distinction to determine how they spend their time. However, it still doesn't entirely solve the problem. Even after listing only what is important in your life, the list often is still too long. Your list may sound something like this:

- be a good parent, spouse, daughter/son, and friend

- produce excellent results on multiple projects at work

- exercise regularly

- eat right

- keep your weight down

- look good

- have a beautiful house

- get your golf handicap down to a level that isn't embarrassing

These things are all important and you'd like to excel at all of them if you had enough time and energy. Well, you *don't* have that much time and energy—no one does. Therefore, you still have more tough choices to make. Even in the areas that are important to you, you must eliminate some things or at least reduce your expectations. For example, several people mentioned that they cannot maintain as many friendships as they wish. They didn't have the time to stay in touch with some old friends, so regretfully those friendships faded to the background of their lives. Others said they were not able to exercise as often as they wanted to or spend time on important hobbies and home projects.

One woman interviewed admitted that she had a very long list of things that mattered to her (e.g., family, friends, work).

> Then I started playing golf. And, of course, I approached golf just like I do everything else. I wanted to be good at it, so I signed up for regular lessons, set a goal for myself to play at least twice a week, and tried to get to the driving range to practise regularly. One day I was out playing and hit a really bad shot. I started to get upset about it and suddenly the thought hit me: "What are you doing to yourself—are you nuts?" I am at the peak of my career and have a very full life. Why am I putting pressure on myself to add "excellent golfer" to the equation at this point? I decided right then and there that golf was going to be one of those areas of my life where mediocre is good enough.

TIP THREE

Making the distinction between the "big rocks" and the "little stuff" won't solve all your problems. You probably still have too many things on the "important" list to excel at all. You still have more choices to make. You'll likely have to lower your expectations in some areas of your life that you value highly.

Don't Sweat the Petty Stuff and
Don't Pet the Sweaty Stuff

Many stories people told us about keeping things in perspective focused on the importance of the "big rocks" in their lives, such as family and friends, success in work or school, and health issues. However, they also talked about keeping track of what really matters in the practical details of their daily lives. Margaret Fisher, strategic planning consultant, quoted one of her favorite lines from comedian George Carlin: "Don't sweat the petty stuff and don't pet the sweaty stuff." She then explained: "At the end of the day, ask yourself 'Did something get accomplished that needed to be accomplished?' It's a binary question—yes or no. If the answer is 'yes,' what needed to happen did happen. That's it. Let go of it and move on. You can go round and round second-guessing the little stuff."

The "little stuff" included all sorts of practical details of daily life from a clean house to micromanaging at work. Bridget Brandt, marketing director of a credit union, said, "My advice is to not let the small things bother you. I work on that every day. At work, we have a lot of micromanagement, so it's important to not let the small things bother me. For example, it makes me crazy that my husband doesn't close the shower curtain, but I have decided not to fight with him over it. In the grand scheme of things, it's really not a big deal." Amy Turner, a human resources representative, explained how she balances the roles of wife, full-time employee, and MBA student when she said, "I've let some things go. I realized that they really didn't matter. Once I said to myself that I can't do everything, I could just go to bed and leave the dishes dirty. The next morning it's okay."

A unit commander in the U.S. Army Reserve talked about the practical issue of dealing with multiple priorities at work:

> I would attend conferences where I would receive briefings from all the staff sections: personnel, security, training, logistics, recruiting, and safety. All of these areas were represented by competent, sincere individuals with tunnel vision. Each staff section would offer chart after chart, explaining why their narrow area of interest should be my number one priority. In these meetings the difference between a staff officer and a unit commander was evident. The unit commander is responsible for everything the unit does or does not do. The staff officer is only interested in his area. As a unit commander, you need to select the important items to improve your unit and be willing to take the heat for not doing everything the staff wants.

TIP FOUR	Identify the "little stuff" in your life. Everyone has an overwhelming number of practical details in his or her daily life that must be managed. You can't get all the details done. Decide what can slide.

Stick to Your Standards

Ethical standards are your internal guidance system, which functions much like the way gyroscopes used to stabilize aircraft and ships. Sticking to your standards and saying "no" to something unethical may be stressful at that time, but in the long run those standards keep your life on course. Sterling Colton, a retired Marriott International executive, described the importance of standards in his life. "It has been helpful to me to have a good lodestar to know where I was going, who I was, and to have standards, so I didn't have to make decisions as to what was right and wrong in many areas. I had made those decisions a long time ago."

Lowell Inkley, a former vice president of a retail chain of photo stores, talked about the peace of mind that comes from sticking to one's standards: "If you're always doing and operating the way you think is the proper way to operate, then you don't get in much trouble. If you are ethical in business, you don't have to worry. You can sleep nights. You can look in the mirror in the morning. You don't have to worry."

If you have a reputation for sticking to your standards, people trust you and work more easily with you. People in family-owned businesses know that an ethical reputation can carry across generations. Rick Woodbury, a real estate developer, talked about how standards were passed down from generation to generation in his family's business.

> I was trying to broker a real estate deal, and another broker was creating all sorts of obstacles for me. In the middle of the negotiation, the seller said, "Well Mr. Woodbury, what do you think about this?" The other broker looked around and said, "Are you Wally's son?" When I said "yes," it changed the whole negotiation. The door was open. All of a sudden they got cooperative. We didn't have to deal with a lot of distrust, and we reached a fair agreement. That was a legacy that my grandfather and my father gave to me. I hope that I am preserving it.

Keep Your Eye on the Prize

Several interviewees used the expression "Keep your eye on the prize" to stress how important it is to stay focused on what matters most to you. Robert Mikesh, an environmental investigator and an MBA student, describes how he gets a grip and avoids burnout by keeping his eye on the prize: "In my work I can help solve somebody's environmental problem, so it gives me something tangible I can get out of my job. It makes me feel good. I also have a plan. I will get my MBA and hopefully get a better job where my wife can stay home with the kids. It lays out in front of us." Joe Galuszka, a cancer survivor, emphasized personal life forces in the story of his cancer struggle. He cited three things that he did simultaneously to deal with his cancer. "You need to completely mobilize and take all human action possible, which includes the best doctors, hospital, and treatment. You also need to have an incredibly strong desire to live, which for me was my wife and two daughters. And then you need to put yourself in God's hands, pray, and believe in a positive outcome. I believe that you must do all of these things together simultaneously; I don't believe they work independently."

Keep Your Options Open

When times get tough, you're less likely to burn out if you feel you have choices. One interviewee put it this way: "You need to actively shape the game you play; don't just play the game you find yourself in." Feeling trapped without options makes you a prime candidate for burnout. Matthew Dunn, the chief information officer for Intrawest in Vancouver, British Columbia, said, "The times I have come close to the edge of burnout have always been rooted in the question, 'Why do I continue to do this?' There have always been alternatives." One corporate director described her method of shaping the game she played during a corporate reorganization:

> I decided to try to build the job I wanted instead of just fitting into what was available. I didn't start out that way, and it put me in a panic. Then I said, "No, take a step back and think about what you really want to do. What's going to make you want to get up in the morning?" If I had just crumbled and said, "Woe is me," I

would not have gotten the job I ended up with. I literally had to carve one out in order to get a job I wanted.

TIP ONE	Actively shape the game you play; don't just play the game you find yourself in. Generate numerous options so you have choices when confronted with tough times.

Ask Yourself What You Don't Want

Knowing what you *don't* want out of life is as helpful as knowing what you want. Tim Aynesworth, is an architect who has lived in Houston and Austin. He was driving to work in 1982, and in the space of a block he counted twenty-three construction cranes. Tim said to himself, "I think it's even possible to overbuild Houston." Then I started scheming. I looked around and thought, "I don't really like Houston much and I don't want to raise my daughter here. What do I miss?" What I missed was rocks and trees, parks and views, nice neighborhoods, and less traffic." He could find all these things if his family moved to Austin, but Austin was a much smaller town and wouldn't offer the opportunities for a "big, hot career." He would have to change his career direction and work for a developer. Tim decided that he wanted the things he missed more than a big career in Houston. He then asked himself, "What if I go to Austin and it doesn't work?" His answer was, "I'd rather be sitting in a rocking chair at the nursing home someday saying that I tried to do it and couldn't rather than saying that I wished I'd tried to do it. I'm going to switch careers." At this point, Tim started developing his options in a new direction. He moved to Austin about a year later and started a new career.

> **TIP TWO**
>
> Knowing what you *don't* want is as important as knowing what you want. Be sure the options you generate are taking you in a direction that you want to go.

A Four-Step Process for Building Your Options

Many individuals talked about the importance of generating options in their lives, even during good times. For example, a number of people working in corporations mentioned that they always were working on options for their next job move, even though they were happy with their current jobs. When describing how they built and evaluated their options, four pieces of advice came up repeatedly:

1. Develop a vision for your life.
2. Conduct continuous environmental scanning.
3. Build a portfolio of options.
4. Be prepared to change.

Step One: Develop a Vision for Your Life

Having a vision of how you want to live is the starting point for generating options. To develop a vision, you don't have to nail down all the details as though you were writing a movie script. Often a vision is a general idea of what you want out of life. Tim

Aynesworth knew he wanted to move from Houston to Austin for what he considered a better quality of life, but it took a year to get the details in place and make the move. Shana Pate Moulton, a university professor who is married and the mother of two children under the age of three, bases her life on a simple vision: "Follow your passion. You have to do what you are passionate about. Then it doesn't seem like work." According to Ginna Gemmell, president and founder of GlidePath®, Inc., one thing that keeps her from burning out is a life goal she developed very early in life:

> Growing up in Appalachia, I made up my mind that I would have an interesting life and that it would be more interesting than anybody around me. I knew that it would require leaving my hometown and striking out on my own to see what I could do. I didn't have a life goal to make a lot of money or to be famous. It was to have an interesting life and be a part of creating something new that would benefit the world, and that has stayed with me through a long career. There is always something engaging and interesting ahead just waiting to be discovered.

Some people's visions are more specific. One interviewee had a dream of being a high school coach. He never let go of this dream, even though his career took him in a different direction and he never acquired the necessary teaching certificate. He always looked for opportunities to work with kids and coach. Over the years, he volunteered as a coach at the high school level and taught at the college level. He concluded, "In a sense I was able to fulfill the dream of being a coach." Some interviewees said they wanted to lead a happy and healthy life or retire to a warm climate where they can play golf every day. Others dreamed of being the chief executive officer of a company or starting their own business. It doesn't matter if your vision is specific or general, grand or simple. What matters is that you have some sense of where you're headed so that you will know which paths might get you there. The purpose of generating options is to give yourself as many paths as possible to your vision.

TIP THREE

Develop a vision of how you want to live. Even if you aren't a good dreamer or an experienced planner, you'll need at least a general sense of what you want. Then you can start generating options that increase the chances of realizing your dream.

Step Two: Conduct Continuous Environmental Scanning

"Environmental scanning" was the term one person used to describe the practice of paying attention to what's going on in your world. This isn't a one-time event or something you start doing when times get tough—it's an ongoing process. Environmental scanning is a lifelong habit of watching the external world around you and examining what's going on inside you.

External Scanning

Scanning the world around you involves learning about events, people, cultures, and occupations that go far beyond your normal day-to-day life. Ashwin Patel, a business and finance executive, explained the importance of expanding your horizons through environmental scanning:

> Think of it as looking through binoculars first, then move on to a telescope, and then look at the world through the Hubbell telescope. Ninety percent of what you see you may not understand, but it will expand your thinking, and the ten percent you do understand will help you tie what you learn back to reality so you can use it. Always keep a telescope in your hand.

Craig Park, a senior executive in the building industry, described his environmental scanning method:

> I like a lot of different perspectives as I collect data. It goes back to my training as an architect. I was trained to gather a lot of information about a particular problem or challenge that I am trying to address and then filter it, filter it, and filter it until right at the very end, the creative piece kicks in and the solution comes out. I gather a lot of information before I finally make the commitment to a choice.

Worst-case planning is another way to do external scanning. One person interviewed described his experiences in the army:

> The U.S. Army Rangers are very effective at using worst-case planning for environmental scanning and keeping their options open. We would evaluate each course of action and determine what the worst thing that could go wrong was. Then we'd plan what we needed to do to overcome that obstacle. You always have choices and options.

A woman who has worked for several well-known technology companies in public relations and advertising described the practical value of paying attention to the environment:

> In my position, I need to pay attention so that I will be able to correctly position the advertising to explain the company's position in the market. When the technology market changed from large computers to personal computers, I needed to change the company's advertising. I use the same techniques to make sure my skills are current and relevant so I will have choices. I need to read this market and know my options in case the company decided to downsize because of the market shift.

TIP FOUR	Make a habit of scanning the world around you to help generate many ideas and options. Don't just pay attention to what's going on in your profession or community. You'll have a much wider range of options if you draw ideas from the larger world.

Internal Scanning

Internal scanning starts with making an inventory of your skills and comparing it to the skills you'll need to achieve your vision. Once you identify the gaps, you can start developing those skills. Chad Reese, a manager in a union environment and a university teacher, wants to be a college professor. To achieve this vision, he needs to complete work on his Ph.D. He is currently working full-time during the day, taking two classes a semester toward his doctorate, and teaching two courses a semester as an adjunct professor. Chad can do this without burning out because it's leading to his dream job. His internal scanning started when he asked himself, "What do I want to be five years from now? What do I need to do to get ready to do that? I don't want to say five years from now, 'I should have done this or I should have done that.' I need to get ready."

Bonnie Barrett, a director at a large pharmaceutical company, talked about the importance of constantly learning about yourself:

> I'm a big believer in changing roles and responsibilities about every three to four years, depending on where you are on the learning curve. It helps me gain insight into myself. I also like the personality measures like Myers-Briggs or the Gallup Strengths-Based assessment. Every time I go through one of those, I gain additional insight that helps me pinpoint my next career move. I think this helps me better position myself and avoid being bored or burnt out.

Andy Goodman, a communications consultant to nonprofits and foundations, described internal scanning as a process of ignoring all the noise around you and trying to hear the voice within that is telling you, "This is really what I love doing." Andy then said:

> I had some voices in my head growing up that told me I wanted to be a lawyer. Unfortunately, those voices belonged to my mother and father. They had me ticketed for law school right up through college, so I took the law boards and one summer I went to work in a law firm, and it was the dullest place on earth. When I went to college, I worked at a campus radio station, and I felt just this tingling. This was exciting; this was fun. If you

listen to the external voices, which start off as your parents and then become things like money and prestige and the acceptance of your peers, it can keep you from hearing your own internal voice. That voice is there, but you consciously have to shut out external voices because they can very easily drown out your true internal voice.

TIP FIVE	Pay attention to what's going on inside you. Shut out the noise around you and listen to your own voice.

Step Three: Build a Portfolio of Options

"Always have more than one plan for how you may proceed. Keep correcting course. Having alternatives in which you are confident is essential," said Matthew Dunn, the chief information officer for Intrawest in Vancouver. Ray Rasmussen, sales manager of a software company, pointed out an important factor to keep in mind when you're generating options and considering which ones to pursue:

> Risk and reward are always in balance. If there is a big reward and you don't think there's much risk, you don't understand what you are doing. Everybody needs to understand what risks they are taking in order to get the rewards they are after. For example, there are a lot of people who are buying cars and houses and spending big bucks on something because it makes them feel really good today. But they are signing up for a long-term risk. If they really sat down and thought about it, they might not do it.

> **TIP SIX**
>
> Remember that reward and risk are always in balance. If you think you've generated options that have a high reward and low risk, you don't understand what you're doing.

Tim Aynesworth, the architect who moved from Houston to Austin, described how he dealt with the economic downturn that hit Austin hard a few years after his move. The development company he was working for went bankrupt and he was left to rebuild his career for a second time. Tim started by generating options:

> I spent the first thirty days on the phone calling everybody I knew. In the meantime, I was reading everything I could get my hands on. I figured out pretty quickly that no one was hiring architects. So who in the heck were they hiring? I decided I was going to find out. In the first couple of months, I set up about forty face-to-face meetings with people and asked them lots of questions about what they were having problems with. I talked to savings and loan people, appraisers, developers, contractors, leasing agents, and just anybody. Then I looked at what they told me and asked myself, "What can I do to help these people?" The next month I went back to see all the ones I thought were reasonable prospects and told them, "This is what I can do for you." I got my first little job for $250. I didn't turn anything down. I made my house payment and just kept going month to month.

Tim eventually built a thriving business providing a much broader range of services than is normally associated with an architect.

	Generate lots of options, not just one or two alternatives. Use everything you learned in environmental scanning to help generate the ideas. Don't get stuck in thinking of yourself only in terms of who you were or what you did in the past.
TIP SEVEN	

Step Four: Be Prepared to Change

Always be ready to change. Margaret Fisher, a strategic planning consultant and formerly of AARP, described her approach as a consultant when working with a client: "My experiences underscore the principle that you must always be ready to change. Things often go differently than planned. You need tools to handle the changes required. Make sure you are always prepared and always have the tools that you need with you." This advice doesn't apply just to consulting—it applies to life in general.

Many interviewees talked about the need to be constantly prepared to change. Ken Kundis, a marketing director for a major corporation, said, "I never have to update my resume. It's always ready. I look at Monster.com every week. It's more of a mental exercise and a desire to remain current regarding my industry than actually looking for a job." Gene Raphaelian, management consultant, said, "Don't be afraid to learn new skills. Put yourself in a position of discomfort after you have been successful in one area." You must mentally prepare to change if the need arises.

One technique described by an interviewee was to periodically list the things you like about your situation and the things you don't like. When the list of things you don't like is longer, it's time to change. Making the list puts you in the frame of mind to change if necessary. Having options means you've defined choices that allow you make things happen rather than having things happen to you. Averil Waters, an attorney who has lived and worked in three different countries, said, "I think one thing that has always been important to me is that I've had an escape route of sorts...in my mind. I may never use it, but it keeps me from feeling boxed in."

Jim Lunsford, training and recruitment director for Wayne Brothers, Inc., summed up the process for keeping your options open: "Don't stay too long doing the same thing. Have a firm, long-range plan with short-term options so when unexpected or uncontrollable events pop up, you are able to deal with them."

TIP EIGHT	Be prepared to change course because life never goes the way you plan. If you're in the habit of generating options, it will be easier to change quickly with less risk of burnout.

CHECKLIST FOR KEEPING YOUR OPTIONS OPEN

Ask yourself the following questions to help develop your options:

Step One: Develop a vision for your life.

What are three of four important things you want out of life? (Your ideas can be specific or general.)

What do you not want out of life? (Knowing what you don't want can be as helpful in steering your life as knowing what you do want.)

Step Two: Conduct continuous environmental scanning— external and internal.

External scanning: What do you do (or can start doing) to learn about events, people, cultures, and occupations outside your normal day-to-day life?

Internal scanning: What do you do (or can start doing) to learn more about yourself and realistically assess your skills and preferences?

Step Three: Build a portfolio of options.

Take your answers in Step One and generate multiple options about how you might accomplish each important goal. Use your answers in Step Two to help you generate those ideas and get input from friends and colleagues.

What are the risks and rewards of each of the options you generate? Remember that risks and rewards are always in balance (greater potential reward goes with greater risk).

Step Four: Be prepared to change.

What mental exercises can you practise regularly to keep you prepared to change? (Examples: Scan Monster.com regularly; dream up possible "escape routes"; change daily routines frequently; and update your resume.)

Make a list of the things you like about your current situation and the things you don't like. What can you do to change the situation so you can improve the balance?

Be Careful How You Tell Your Own Story

Everyone's life is a story. The same events can be told as a hero's tale or a victim's account. Your life can be cast as an adventure or a disaster. Events can be funny or tragic. It all depends on the telling. One person interviewed put it this way: "If you see yourself as a victim, then you are a victim. The story becomes true for you the more you tell it."

TIP ONE	Be careful how you tell your own story because you're the one who must live with it.

Storytelling is the most powerful form of human communication. People remember information longer if it's delivered as a story. They also believe the information more readily when it's in this form as opposed to simple facts and figures. In an organization, the ripple effect of a story is a powerful force for shaping people's opinions of events. If most stories about the company are cynical and depressing, morale is much lower than in a setting where a large percentage of the stories are more hopeful. The types of stories told affect the overall "health" of the organization; exactly the same thing is true with individuals. How you tell your own story affects your ability to avoid burnout.

What's Your Story?

Many people don't see their life as a story. They say, "I don't have any stories to tell. My family never told stories." Those same people then tell story after story about their lives. When this is pointed out, they say, "Those aren't stories. Those are just events from my life." When conducting our interviews, we found that many individuals respond more easily to "Can you give me an example of that?" rather than "Can you tell me a story about that?" Your life is a story, and you're the author. It's an autobiography, and you have control over how you relate the tale. You may not be able to control all events that happen to you, but you certainly control the interpretation of the events, the tone, and the moral of the story.

TIP TWO

Start thinking of your life as a story rather than simply a long chain of events. It's an autobiography, and you're the author whether or not you ever write it down. Make sure you "write" a story that doesn't depress you.

Are You a Hero or a Victim in Your Story?

There are a number of variables in how you tell your story, but the most important one for avoiding burnout is whether you cast yourself in the role of hero or victim. Spending your life as a victim is exhausting and depressing. Burning out is probably inevitable for people who see themselves in the victim role. On the other hand, seeing yourself as a hero overcoming obstacles can inspire you to accomplish amazing feats.

The story of the hero is one of the oldest forms of storytelling and mythology. The age-old definition of a hero is someone who takes off on a journey with a goal. The hero is often pitted against insurmountable odds or an adversary with whom he or she must do battle. There is no certainty that the hero will succeed or even survive the journey. We have distorted the idea of heroes in the modern world of movies where the star of the show almost never dies. In the history of mythology and real-world events, there are no such guarantees. Martin Luther King Jr. and Gandhi are two real-life examples of heroes who died while fighting for their causes. Therefore, it would be very easy for a hero to assess the situation and conclude that he or she is being victimized. It's a choice of how you interpret events as they happen to you, not a foregone conclusion based on the facts of the situation. King chose the theme "I Have a Dream" for his famous speech. If he had delivered an eloquent speech called "I Am a Victim," it's unlikely that it would be remembered as one of history's greatest speeches.

You don't have to be famous to see your life in heroic terms. Ashwin Patel, a business and finance executive, made this choice early in his career. Ashwin was an accounting student in Leicester, England, when he bet his flat mate that he would become a partner at a major accounting firm before his friend. What made this bet particularly daunting was that there had never been an Indian partner in a major accounting firm. As an Indian who had grown up in Africa and received most of his education in England, Ashwin already had faced discrimination many times. He knew what he was up against. However, he made the bet anyway. During his job hunt after graduation, he received rejection after rejection in the mail while his flat mate was getting interviews and job offers. But Ashwin kept going. He knew what it would take for him to succeed: "You have to stay two steps ahead of everyone else, put in a helluva lot of hours, keep proving yourself, and expanding your expertise into new areas." At the age of twenty-nine he was made partner at KPMG (Peat Marwick Mitchell at that time). He was one of the youngest people to reach that goal and the firm's first Indian partner. Telling the story almost thirty years later, he grinned when he announced the best part of the story—he won the bet.

There are dozens of ways that Ashwin could have viewed his circumstances. The way he related the story of his early career indicates how he tells his entire autobiography. Now, in his late fifties, he could easily retire and rest on his laurels. His friends kid him that they expect to get an e-mail someday soon saying, "Gone to New Zealand!" However, after retiring from Ernst & Young (another major firm that he joined after fifteen years with KPMG), he went on to work as a CFO for a nonprofit association. He is still learning and stretching his skills, putting in long hours, and contributing to something he believes is important.

TIP THREE

No matter how tough the circumstances, cast yourself as the hero of your story, not the victim. It increases the odds of success and decreases the danger of burning out.

Is the Tone of Your Story Funny or Tragic?

One interviewee put it this way:

> I have started telling my story over the last couple of years during all my life changes (corporate mergers and divorce) by e-mailing certain friends. I often start the message with the reminder that "He who laughs at himself first beats others to the punch." I'm usually able to turn the events into something funny. I don't want pity. I want to tell people what's going on and maybe ask them for advice. But I don't want gloom and doom. Even little things like the time I walked around all day at work with a sticker stuck on my butt. That could have been totally humiliating, but I made it into something funny.

Jane Mobley is a survivor of ovarian cancer and at the time of the interviews was undergoing treatment for breast cancer. She recently had a double mastectomy and described her new look in her characteristically funny way: "I rather like my new figure. It is very aerodynamic. I look like a marathon runner— but without the sweat."

TIP FOUR

Humor helps makes the rough times bearable.

What's the Moral of Your Story?

Storytelling is a powerful teaching tool. In tribes, families, and communities, stories are one of the most common ways the elders teach the values of the group to its members. This is a most effective tool for passing on their group's culture. A Native American woman described her memories of how her grandfather used stories: "He was a tribal elder, and he told lots of stories about the heritage of our tribe. He would always end a story with the words, 'And the reason we still tell that story is…' and then he would go on to explain the meaning of the story to our tribe." In other words, he explained the moral of the story.

Julie Freeman, president of the International Association of Business Communicators, recounted a funny story told by a previous boss. It's a lighthearted story, but it has a moral to it. "He had a boss who used to give him projects and say, 'Now, Ron, this needs to go on the front burner.' Then a couple days later he'd give him another project and say again, 'This needs to go on the front burner.' This went on for awhile, and finally Ron turned to his boss and said, 'How big a stove do you think I have?'" Julie uses the story to illustrate how easily everything becomes a priority. "I often think we are too quick to say 'Yes, I'll take care of that.'" And her last sentence is the moral to the story.

> Identify the moral of your story. Don't assume that it's obvious to other people. Stories are a powerful teaching tool. Be clear about the message you want your story to carry.

Have You Created a Superhero Reputation for Yourself?

Many of our interviewees are high achievers who invested massive amounts of time, energy, and enthusiasm into accomplishing their goals. Even people who were still in their twenties had already developed impressive reputations. These are people you could count on to carry a heavy load of responsibility, never let you down, and accomplish amazing feats. Looking at the transcripts from the interviews, you could conclude that they are an unusual group of superheroes with special talents for success. The problem with this assumption is that it's wrong. Their stories include the usual number of layoffs, illnesses, divorces, frustrating job situations, and children who drive them nuts at times. They're not superheroes. Some talked about the dangers of getting trapped in a "bionic" reputation. This reputation can set the bar so high for future performance and demand such a constant pace of extraordinary efforts and outcomes that it's impossible to maintain. An autobiography that casts you as superhero is dangerous and can lead to burnout.

Averil Waters is an English lawyer who has worked in England, Hong Kong, and Australia in a succession of high-pressure jobs. She described the struggle to learn her limits at work.

Things can be happening that you don't really notice, and the pressures are building up. A classic one for me was when I had been in Hong Kong for about three years and took on a new role. It was quite demanding, and I hadn't done it before. None of us really knew what would be involved in the new job when I started the work. I got more and more stressed, but didn't realize it was happening. Then one night I had a dream that someone was climbing in the window with a knife and coming to stab me. It was a tremendously vivid dream. When I woke up, I knew the dream was about work. And I thought to myself, this is silly—it's too much. I went in the next day and showed my boss what I was working on, and he was shocked. He got someone in to help me. You have to learn not to be scared to say, 'I can't do it.' And that's hard. You expect so much of yourself.

One of the interviewees gave a humorous description of the never-ending struggle of choosing where to put your time and energy:

You don't have enough time for everything, so you devote your energy to what demands the most time at that moment. When that piece is satisfied, you move on to the next thing. And when nothing extreme happens, the stress isn't overwhelming. But things happen that throw it out of balance. For example, I have two children with special needs and that takes an exceptional amount of time and energy. Or when I'm trying to manage my personal life and there is a crisis at work

... It throws life all out of balance. I describe it this way: Life is a seesaw. And if you have the right amount weight on each end, you are in balance. Then sometimes it is weighted more heavily on one end. Even that's manageable. And then sometimes, the seesaw falls off the base and that's just too much!

And she laughed. Many people interviewed had the drive to do great things and lead complex, demanding lives. But sometimes the seesaw falls off the base and at that point it's probably a good idea to stop for a minute and laugh.

TIP SIX	Manage your reputation. It's great to be known as a high achiever whom everyone can count on. However, you're the one who must set the pace and limits. And sometimes you just have to stop and laugh.

PART TWO

Habits and Actions

One day a friend asked Will Rogers if he only had forty-eight hours to live, how would he live them. The cowboy philosopher laughed and replied, "One at a time."

Thoughts and attitudes without actions to back them up don't produce much. In this section, our interview subjects tell us when, where, and how they take action to prevent burnout.

Early in my career I did it wrong. The more difficult the times got, the harder I worked. I had the attitude that I needed to do it myself, stay in control, or it wouldn't get done. I had a hard time sleeping, so I got up at 5 a.m. every day to start working. I did that day after day. Fortunately, I learned the "woes of my ways." How do I deal with it today? In two ways. First, I came to realize the importance of a solid, capable staff and effective delegation. The "one man show" routine is neither effective nor healthy for the long run. Second, you must have the discipline to build time off into your schedule. A balance between work and personal life is extremely important. It's too easy to get caught in the endless cycle of working and never stop. Now in the winter I make time to snowmobile with my sons, in the summer I ride motorcycles, and, most importantly, I make sure I

schedule and take all vacation time. Sometimes when I get off an airplane, all I can think about is getting my suit off, putting on my jeans and boots, and taking a ride on my motorcycle to relieve the stresses of the day.
— *Jim Guidici, executive vice president, BISYS*

Taking yourself too seriously is an absolute recipe for burnout. No question about it. I definitely fall into the laugh camp.
—*Nate Gatten, financial services lobbyist*

There is an old expression, "The devil is in the details." The wisdom of this saying certainly holds true when it comes to habits and actions. People's successes are based on the details of their rituals and habits. These individuals don't wait until they are in danger of burning out to take emergency action. They live in a continual state of *not* burning out.

The people we interviewed don't rely on innate talents or personality predispositions. Many talked about long, hard struggles to learn these behaviors and incorporate them into their lives. Almost all said that their current successes were built on past failures from which they learned valuable lessons. It takes discipline and practice, not luck or talent, to develop a pattern of living that keeps you from burning out.

Laugh More Than You Whine

Whining and complaining are worse than a waste of energy and time. They are a fast track to burnout. The more you do it, the worse you feel mentally and physically. On the other hand, a good laugh makes you feel better. One of the most important habits for avoiding burnout is to substitute laughing for complaining whenever you can. An exceptional sense of humor is not required to put this habit into practice. Many people we interviewed were not great comedians. They would never make a living on the comedy circuit. That's not the point. What's important is that these people laugh a lot and whine very little.

Chad Reese, a manager in a union environment and a university teacher, pointed out that laughter does more than help you avoid burning out: "Laughter energizes you, and that ends up energizing the people around you. That is something I depend on a lot . . . laughter and lightheartedness. When you come to work, it's got to be fun. If it's not fun, it's the wrong job. You need to find something fun that you can enjoy every day."

In 1,000 pages of interview transcripts for this book, it is difficult to find complaints. These people have survived plenty of complaint-worthy events. They experienced the usual number of daily irritants and the occasional catastrophe, but they didn't complain. The point of the interviews was to find stories of times when they should have burnt out but didn't. So we invited them to spend an hour reliving hard times in their lives—and still they didn't complain. Sometimes they told us about painful times when they burnt out and then pulled themselves back together—even then there wasn't any complaining. Some related the stories in a matter-of-fact, clipped way, while others wove more drama into the telling. However, there was never a woe-is-me tone to the story, and they quickly moved on to talk about what they learned or how they got themselves out of a bad situation.

Laugh at Things That Aren't Funny

A hilarious story recently passed anonymously on the Internet from one woman to another. The subject of the story wasn't funny. It was one woman's experience of getting a mammogram. Anyone who has had this procedure will tell you it is not a funny process. This woman's experience was worse than usual—the machine caught on fire during the procedure. However, even though the topic is unpleasant, painful, and potentially dangerous, her telling of the story is an absolute riot. Here are a few lines from her story. She was in the middle of the procedure when the technologist yelled, "Oh no!"

These are, perhaps, the words you least want to hear from any health professional. Suddenly, she came flying past me, her lab coat whipping behind her, on her way out the door. She yelled over her shoulder, "The machine's on fire, I'm going to get help!" Okay, I was wrong. "The machine's on fire" are the worst words you can hear from a health professional. Especially if you're all alone and semipermanently attached to A MACHINE and don't know if it's THE MACHINE in question. I struggled for a few seconds trying to get free, but even Houdini couldn't have escaped. I decided to go to plan B: yelling at the top of my lung (the one that was still working). I hadn't seen anything on fire, so my panic hadn't quite reached epic proportions. But then I started to smell smoke coming from behind the partition. This is ridiculous, I thought. I can't die like this. What would they put in my obituary? Cause of death: Breast entrapment?

Whoever wrote this has a real gift for telling a funny story. Not everyone can tell a story so well that it hits the Internet and spreads like wildfire, but everyone can form the habit of choosing to laugh instead of complain.

TIP ONE | Don't wait for something funny to happen to you. Choose to laugh at yourself and the hard knocks of life instead of complaining, ranting, or whining.

Use Humor to Connect with People and Make a Point

Bob Kulbick, an executive in the insurance industry, took over the leadership of a company at a time when many employees were very unhappy with the disruption and uncertainty going on around them. He visited each office and often faced a hostile audience of employees who had never met him and were not in the mood to give him the benefit of the doubt. Bob often used humor to connect with the employees and make a point about how the new company would be run. One time he was asked about the old, unpopular dress code. Rather than give a detailed, factual explanation of the changes in the rules, he simply said, "Well, I'll tell you one thing; I'm not wearing pantyhose to work anymore!" Everyone laughed, and they got the point.

Bob's most dramatic use of humor occurred at the New York City office. Employees were very upset about a number of recent policy changes, and you could feel the tension as about 100 staff members came into the large conference room to meet the new boss. There is nothing quite like a group of New Yorkers in a bad mood. Everyone but Bob was worried about how the meeting would go. He was in his usual upbeat mood. At these meetings, Bob was usually the second speaker on the agenda, but that day he wanted to go first. He walked out in front of the group, told the audience who he was, and said, "I hear you've been told that you can't have spring water in the offices anymore and you aren't allowed to eat in the building cafeteria from now on." There were a few nods and a lot of glares from the audience. Then he said, "Well, I just want to say this first. You can have your water back and you can eat in the cafeteria." The crowd erupted in applause and laughter. He held up his hands to quiet them and said, "I just have to tell you one more thing. That water is expensive, so we'll be removing the toilet paper from the restrooms to make up for the cost." And they roared with laughter. Bob just stood there grinning. He didn't have to explain that he thought the policy decisions about water and lunch were silly and that he didn't like silly policies. Everyone got the message. He also won them over. The employees were grinning as they left the meeting and clearly felt like there was some hope for this company after all.

TIP TWO	Use humor to make a point. Making people laugh creates a connection between the speaker and listener and drives home the point in a way that facts and figures never do.

Allow Yourself Self-Pity Breaks

Everyone needs a good gripe or whine sometimes. Years ago a woman in her seventies was interviewed in a major news magazine. She was still an active hiker and climber long past the age when most people had retired to less strenuous activities. She had much the same attitude as those interviewed for this book. This woman made sure she kept her thoughts and attitudes positive and complained very little. However, she did have one habit that didn't fit the mold. She allowed herself ten minutes a day for self-pity. For that time, she really let go and ranted and whined up a storm to herself. At the end of the ten minutes, the pity break was over. Those thoughts were put aside, and her life proceeded using her characteristically positive approach.

Shana Pate Moulton, a university professor with a background in elementary school teaching, told about a group of teachers who became friends:

> I think it's very important to have friends at work because it gives you a group with whom you can whine for a few minutes, but also a group with whom you can bond. When you have the same experience, it is helpful because you are all living through the same thing. There were ten of us third grade teachers. We had our gritching moments, but then we decided to stop eating lunch in the teachers' lounge, so we would hear only ourselves and not the complaining of the other teachers. We would gripe for a few minutes, and then we would literally say, "Stop. No more. What are you guys doing this weekend? How's your son doing in school?" We just talked about other things or the successes with our classes. It's important sometimes to get the whining out and to just bitch for a while. Get it out and then let it go. But you have to let it go.

TIP THREE	Take a ten-minute self-pity break each day. Then get over it and move on with your life using a positive attitude.

Another interviewee uses these types of breaks after receiving unexpected bad news. It often helps to take a break to let the news sink in and rant or cry. Her favorite breaks are lying on the living room floor or walking by the lake near her house. She said the place she picks depends on how melodramatic she is planning to be. Attracting attention to herself at the lake is not really helpful. She cautioned not to let these breaks last too long. Depending on the magnitude of the bad news, anywhere from a few minutes to an hour is probably enough. At that point, it's better to shift into action mode and start working out the steps for dealing with the problem. Her most vivid memory of one break was the time her doctor called and told her she had cancer. "That crying jag on the living room floor lasted at least an hour," she said. She quickly pointed out that in extreme situations, one crying jag wouldn't be enough. However, her point was to move on fairly quickly to thinking about the next steps. This is key to coping well with the most difficult situations.

> **TIP FOUR**
>
> The unexpected bad news break is a variation of the ten-minute self-pity break. Take time for ranting or crying. Then switch gears and focus on thinking about the next steps for dealing with the problem.

Use Humor to Keep Things in Perspective

Linda Goold, a lawyer from Washington, D.C., was comforting a friend going though a divorce. Having had a similar experience, Linda offered the friend the following wisdom: "The good news is that you don't die of it. The bad news is that you don't die of it." Linda's friend burst into laughter and responded, "Oh, how true." There were moments when she wished she would die of it, but sooner or later she knew she would recover. Linda, who is known for a great sense of humor, frequently uses that expression to keep painful events in perspective. The great thing about this saying is that it carries two messages. One message is "Keep it in perspective; it won't kill you." The other message is sympathy; it feels like it will kill you and at times you probably wish it would. During painful times, the only thing better than laughter is laughter combined with kindness and understanding.

TIP FIVE	Use humor to keep the painful events in perspective. "The good news is that you won't die of it. And the bad news is that you won't die of it."

Use Laughter to Blow Off Steam

"I try to take it one day at a time, but sometimes several days attack me all at the same time."[1] Sometimes too many problems and irritants pile on at one time, and the tension builds like a pressure cooker. It's time to blow off some steam. Laughter is a great way to do that. Alice Swearingen, a director at a global pharmaceutical company, credits this kind of laughter with aerobic exercise value: "The group went out to lunch the other day, and we laughed so hard we cried. I'm sure it was an aerobic abdominal exercise. We probably burnt off that cheesecake we shared."

TIP SIX	Laugh to let off steam when the pressure builds up . . . and to burn off cheesecake.

---

[1] Allen, *Getting Things Done*, 5.

Laughter Brings People Together

Shared funny experiences can bring a group of people together and create a team spirit. Margaret Fisher, a strategic planning consultant and formerly of AARP, described one way this can happen:

> One thing I learned at AARP was the ability to create contextual humor or a private joke, if you will. Even in short experiences, it brings the group together. Some humorous piece becomes shorthand for the experience. Everyone is in on the joke. It's like a secret handshake. It's only appropriate for that particular setting, and it lasts only as long as that setting lasts. For example, one time I was on a team where we were working on a very creative project. One team member was a guy whose thinking style was to focus on minute details all the time. We developed this code phrase to use whenever we were starting to work on a particularly creative piece. One of us would announce that the guy "is being paged to the load dock." He was in on the joke and we'd all laugh.

The phrase "being paged to the load dock" was used by the group as a funny way to handle his role on the team. It brought the group together in a situation that could have caused dissension.

Obviously, these "private jokes" can be used in a destructive way that creates a clique, not a team. If humor excludes other people and makes them feel like outsiders, this use of laughter does harm. Margaret hit on the crucial element that keeps this from happening when she said, "Everyone is in on the joke." As long as everyone knows the story and is part of the laughter, you can avoid the insider-outsider problem.

TIP SEVEN	Funny stories, jokes, or phrases shared by a group are a great team builder. Make sure that everyone is in on the joke. Otherwise, you are creating a clique, not a team.

Sometimes work groups use this type of humor to defend themselves in difficult situations. In this case, it often takes the form of gallows humor. One person interviewed talked about working for a toxic boss. She said the employees in that division became a support group to each other:

> We turned our encounters with the boss into humorous experiences or observations. We noticed that she would focus on one person for awhile and then would shift to someone else. So we watched for the shift. We had a phrase for it: "Someone was on the spit." That was the person getting roasted. She inadvertently created quite a strong team, and it had a completely different purpose than what she had intended.

TIP EIGHT	Gallows humor shared by a team can help people protect themselves in a bad situation. This is usually a short-term fix because it probably won't correct the situation. However, it is a way to make that situation more bearable for people while they endure it.

Smiling Works as Well as Laughing

Smile and you feel better. Act like you're in a good mood and your frame of mind improves. Change your actions and trigger a change in your emotions. In Chapter Four, we addressed this same issue about the link between thinking and emotions. Changing your thinking can trigger changes in your mood. When it comes to thoughts, actions, and emotions, people tend to think that emotions are the leading and most powerful factor: "I'm in a bad mood, so my behavior and thoughts match my mood." This certainly can be true, but the opposite is also true. If you have positive thoughts and behave in an upbeat manner, your mood shifts to match those thoughts and actions. It's a two-way street.

Ed Gallagher, a marketing director in the pharmaceutical industry, described it this way: "If you decide you want to be happy and you are going to be happy, then you need to smile. Your mood and your actions cannot be incongruent. So act the way you want to be and you will end up feeling it. Your brain will adjust. You can't just think you want to be happy. You have to start acting happy. Then you'll be happy."

TIP NINE	Act the way you want to be and you end up feeling it. Upbeat behavior triggers a better mood.

Our interviewees and the many experts studying positive emotions agree that facial expressions, especially smiles, are very important triggers of emotions and moods. There are also qualitative differences in smiles. People smiling with their mouths but not their eyes don't get the same mood-elevating effect.

TIP TEN

Facial expressions are especially important. Don't walk around all day with a blank expression or a scowl if you want to be in a good mood. Smile or look happy, and you'll feel better. Use your whole face. Smile with your mouth and eyes. Mouth-only smiles won't improve your mood as much.

chapter 8

If You're a Control Freak, Get Over It

"There is no point in doing well that which you should not be doing at all," said Patricia Fripp.[1] Control freaks not only burn themselves out, they burn out everyone who works or lives around them. They may be very good at getting things done and producing excellent work, but the price paid for those results is very high. One person interviewed described it this way: "Working for a control freak is miserable; being one is even more miserable. It's exhausting." If the leaders in a work setting have high-control management styles, the morale in that organization probably will be low. Micromanaging, as it is often called, usually leads to one of two attitudes: "Why did you bother to hire me if you don't trust anything I do?" (anger and resentment) or, even worse, "Why bother? Nothing we do will satisfy them anyway" (apathy). Cheryl Jernigan, community activist and former association executive, warned about this

---

[1] Richard K. Biggs, *Burn Brightly without Burning Out: Balancing Your Career with the Rest of Your Life* (Nashville: Thomas Nelson Publishers, 2002), 52.

issue: "To some people, control is different than perfectionism, but they are kidding themselves. Some will say, 'I don't control people, but I expect things to be done right.' It's the same thing!"

Wanting to control everything and everybody around you is a tough habit to break, and some individuals interviewed have struggled long and hard to get over it. Their basic personalities haven't changed, but they have learned to keep their control freak tendencies under control . . . most of the time.

TIP ONE

Do not make people change what they are doing unless it is truly necessary. Micromanagers often want things done exactly the way they would do it even if it makes very little difference in the quality of the final outcome.

If You Don't Trust Them, You Can't Delegate to Them

Jeff Jernigan, president and CEO of Union Bank in Kansas City, talked at length about the connection between delegation and trust:

> You need to learn to delegate to avoid burning out, and that means you have to hire people you can delegate to and feel good about doing it. You always inspect what you expect, but you've got to hire people you can trust. One of my main reasons for not burning out is that I hire people who are experts in their fields. I know I can trust them. Hell, I don't work sixty hours a week. I

work forty to fifty hours most weeks. And the reason I can get away and not worry is because I have three people reporting to me who are as good as I am in their areas. So I keep telling our managers, "You've got to cull your staff to where you hire people who you can trust because you can't do it all. You are never going to succeed without staff you can trust."

TIP TWO

Not being a control freak means delegating. That means you must trust the competence and judgment of the people working for you and those on a team with you. Surround yourself with people you trust . . . hire them, train them, and recruit them to your team. If you don't trust them, you never get over being a control freak.

Inspect What You Expect

In Jeff's comments, he mentioned that he "inspects what he expects." He said this more than once in the interview and went on to say, "They know I will be involved in everything they do, but I'm not doing the work or handling the situation myself. In an organization this size, I just can't." This is the piece often missed. Not being a micromanager means delegating work, but it doesn't mean disappearing from the scene. Figuring out how to stay "involved in everything they do" without taking over their work is the balance each person must find. This usually means keeping in touch regularly to stay informed about a project, making suggestions, and checking accuracy or quality at key project milestones. This takes practice to learn when and how often to check in with people.

Here are the comments of Chelsea Shaffer, a twenty-seven-year-old mortgage broker who is still sorting out how to strike this balance with people working in her company:

> It's a fine line. There are certain things in your work that you don't want to give up. For instance, I'm working a loan sell right now. It has our lien position on it. We have to make sure all of our lien positions are correct, all of our insurance is correct, everything is right, so when we sell it, there's no problem. If anything is wrong, we have to buy it back, so we can lose a lot of money. It's a big issue. The control freak part of me just wants to do it myself and make sure it's done right. But I also know I need to let other people learn how to do the work. It's a fine line because there's a lot of money on the line and I have to trust the people I work with and help them learn.

Chelsea is absolutely right. She must ensure that both issues are covered. The work must be done accurately, and she must help her staff learn how to do these tasks themselves. So she has to decide what "inspect what you expect" means in this situation. How can Chelsea let other people do the task and also be involved at several points along the way to make absolutely sure the work going out the door is accurate? Doing it all herself is not the answer, but she can't walk away and keep her fingers crossed that the work will be accurate. Crossing your fingers and hoping isn't a technique that any reformed control freak embraces.

| **TIP THREE** | Inspect what you expect even with people you trust. Identify several milestones throughout a project when you will "get involved" to check if the work is on track. Help people correct the course as they go, but do not take over and do the work. |

Each situation you face will be different. Tomorrow Chelsea will work on a different project, and the balance of how often to monitor the work will be different than it was on the loan sell. There isn't a formula you can follow; it's a judgment call on each project.

| **TIP FOUR** | Be careful you don't have too many milestones when you get involved. Having too many checkpoints is one way control freaks delude themselves that they are delegating when they aren't. |

Don't Take Over When the Team Gets Bogged Down

One reason people jump in and take over is because they think the project is bogged down. To get things moving again, they grab the reins and do everything themselves, or they start barking orders. Taking over may get the group back on track as far as the task is concerned, but it probably undermines the team's morale and confidence. It's usually better to help the group get themselves back on track. One interviewee with years of experience leading teams suggested that often the most important thing you need to do is to build their confidence: "Point out how much they have accomplished, how good the work is so far, and tell them you know they can meet the deadline. Teams sometimes get discouraged in the middle of a project. It doesn't necessarily mean anything is going wrong."

TIP FIVE	When a team (or an individual) gets bogged down, don't jump in and take over. Encourage them and build their confidence that they are doing fine and will be successful if they just keep going. Often all they need is a morale booster.

Another way to help a group right itself is to turn the question, "What's the next step?" into a team ritual. If team members frequently ask themselves this question, it keeps everyone moving forward. Sometimes projects get bogged down because there is so much to do and it starts to seem overwhelming. However, if you keep people focused on the next steps, it prevents them from being paralyzed by the project's size. There is an old adage, "How do you eat an elephant? One bite at a time." Keep a team focused on the next bites, and they will move forward.

TIP SIX	Develop the ritual of asking yourselves and each other the question, "What's the next step?" If you focus on the next action, you are less likely to be overwhelmed by the complexity of the whole project.

Being Overly Helpful Is a Control Freak in Disguise

Sometimes overly helpful behavior is a way of staying in control of a project's details. One woman remembered the time an employee threw her out of his office because she had been coming in too often to "help" on the implementation of a new database project. "He said it like he was joking, but I knew he really meant it. I wasn't helping. I was snooping around to see how things were going. And I was getting on his nerves."

TIP SEVEN

If someone throws you out of his or her office, it probably means you have taken "being helpful" too far. Back off. And laugh at yourself while you're at it.

Sometimes it can be a whole committee of people whose efforts to be helpful turn into interference. When Bob Kulbick was appointed CEO of RSKCo, a newly formed subsidiary of CNA Insurance Company, he ran into a number of cases of micromanaging that were slowing down the new company's ability to get up and running quickly. One group was a twenty-five-person steering committee made up of senior-level people who were supposed to be "steering" the coordination of the start-up activities. Bob attended one of its first meetings and listened to members requesting all sorts of detailed reports and justifications from managers who were trying to get their departments going. As far as he could see, the main thing the committee was doing was slowing down the process and frustrating the managers. When asked what he did about it, Bob responded, "I cancelled the steering committee. That was their last meeting. I got a lot of phone calls from people on the committee who were upset, but the managers didn't need that kind of help."

In another case, Bob and one of his senior people met with the product development committee to decide whether or not to invest money in a new business for the company that involved very expensive trucking equipment. The group kept requesting additional information and justification for the new venture. Each request meant a two- to four-week delay until the next committee meeting. The person trying to run the project was getting more frustrated with each delay. When they walked out of another meeting with another round of requests for more information, the man in charge of the project turned to Bob and said, "I can't believe this. This is driving me crazy." Bob responded, "Don't worry about it anymore. Build the truck. Just do it." How did he deal with the committee that was waiting for the follow-up information? It was simple; Bob never went back to any of their meetings. Three months later when the new truck was unveiled, people just assumed it had been approved. Bob laughed and said, "So many people skip those meetings, they all assumed it was approved at one of the meetings they'd missed." Large bureaucracies often institutionalize micromanaging. Many people who are good at getting things done in these settings are the ones skilled at end-running the system without pushing it so far that they get in trouble.

TIP EIGHT

Learn how and when you can end-run the bureaucracy and "just do it." The old adage "Don't ask permission and apologize later" applies in this situation. However, do not go beyond what's safe for you at your level and experience in the company.

You Can't Always Save the World

Many people we interviewed talked about the importance of making choices. There is one aspect of this that is particularly tough for people with self-confessed control-freak tendencies. Their efforts to control events and people around them often are based on the best of intentions. They have great ideas about wonderful things they want to do. These individuals are sure they can make their ideas happen if they try hard enough—and get everyone else to try hard enough too. Unfortunately, it doesn't always work out as they planned. Many interviewees have great enthusiasm about so many ideas or have ideas on such a grand scale that there is simply no way they can pull them all off successfully no matter how hard they drive themselves or the people around them.

Kelsey August, an entrepreneurial wonder who started three businesses by the age of thirty-four and is the youngest woman to make the Inc. 500 list, talked about "hitting the wall" a few years ago with one of her businesses:

> At twenty-seven, we were at fifty employees, $2 million in sales, and I was the only leader. I hired welfare-to-work employees, women coming into the workforce for the first time, and people who were young with immature skill sets. I had a vision of building a great workforce from this mix of employees. We would all do great things together. And then I hit the wall. I thought I was having a nervous breakdown. That's when I knew I needed to regroup and lead differently. I had to start delegating, but to do that I needed more skilled people working in the company. I had to admit to myself that I couldn't save the world.

After she restructured the company, her role was quite different: "I was still working hard, but it wasn't the 100-hour work weeks I was putting in before."

TIP NINE	If you have great ideas and massive amounts of energy and enthusiasm, don't get delusional. You still have to make choices. You can't drive yourself and the people around you hard enough to succeed at all your grand schemes.

Develop
Healthy Rituals

"Take spontaneous breaks for chocolate, and take someone with you." This is a great example of the advice offered by many interviewees. We thought that exercise, eating right, meditation, and relaxation techniques would be the hot topics. These traditional health activities are undoubtedly important in avoiding burnout; many people interviewed worked hard at incorporating these habits into their lives. However, much of what we heard didn't fit that mold. For example, most books on stress and burnout tell you to cut down on television watching, and yet of one of the most energetic and upbeat individuals we interviewed described himself as a TV freak: "I love going home and watching the tube at night." He exercises regularly and takes good care of himself in many ways, but watching TV is one of his routines for unwinding and relaxing.

Use a Variety of Healthy Rituals to Rejuvenate

What was most striking from the interviews was the variety of rituals or routine behaviors that people used to unwind, recover their energy, and rejuvenate their spirit. In many cases, it wasn't just a matter of a variety of healthy habits from one person to another, but a variety of activities within their individual lives. Many interviewees talked about the need to be constantly prepared to change.

Alice Swearingen, a corporate director, mentioned variety as her first piece of advice on how to keep from burning out. She cautioned not to put 100 percent of your time into work. For her the variety came from her kids and athletics.

TIP ONE	Don't limit your idea of healthy rituals to the traditional categories of exercise, diet, meditation, and relaxation techniques. These are great, but there are hundreds of other activities and habits that help people rejuvenate. Look for new ideas and incorporate a variety of healthy rituals into your life.

Not Your Typical Healthy Rituals

Here are some stories that people recounted about healthy rituals in their lives that don't fit the traditional mold. They ran the gamut from brewing beer to dancing and singing. Ina Lavin talked about doing volunteer work during her nine-month job hunt after she had been laid off:

> I decided I wanted to volunteer. I got involved in The Wellness Community, a social services organization that runs groups for people with cancer. Sometimes when I would go there to volunteer, I'd think I wasn't

doing anything very exciting—just answering the phone. And then one day I was having lunch with a woman who told me she was recovering from breast cancer and started telling me about The Wellness Community. I said, "I'm volunteering there." And she just lit up like a Christmas tree. I felt so good.

Chris McEntee, a health care executive, talked about family rituals. She and her husband, Hank, have a "date" every Wednesday at 6 p.m. "We just spend an hour together, have a drink, and talk. The boys know they can't disturb us. We try not to talk too much about the kids, but I can't say we stick to that very well." They bicycle to church on Sunday mornings when the weather is nice and have dinner in the dining room as a family on Sunday evenings:

> That's a time we sit as a family. We always start meals with a prayer, but on Sunday night we each have to say what we are thankful for from the week. We light the candles, even if the food isn't fancy. We don't really care about that. It could be spaghetti and meatballs. What's important is that we try to make it a family ritual.

One of the interviewees has a high-pressure job as head of human resources for a large Canadian retailer, is raising two children, and is attending graduate school. She talked about the cottage that she and her husband bought and renovated. Her mother thought she was nuts. However, the cottage isn't more work for her—it's a sanctuary. "I love it. I go there, put on my music, and dust. I'm in heaven on earth. The sun sets and life is good." She laughed and admitted that most people wouldn't put dusting high on their list of relaxing activities, but it works for her.

Sometimes it was the enjoyment of the place that people described as rejuvenating. Sterling Colton, retired Marriott International executive, talked about when he and his wife lived in British Columbia, Canada. "We were fortunate to live in a very beautiful part of the world. We both love the outdoors, so being able to travel through the mountains was really therapeutic for us. We saw things we had never seen before like a mother bear and her cubs and a big bull moose. It was rejuvenating."

One person talked about the importance of celebrating victories. He was a program director for a national association who worked with large groups of volunteers all over the country lobbying at state legislatures:

> We celebrated our victories in several ways. One was that every time a bill got passed, I organized a conference call so that everyone could congratulate each other for the good work. Then at the end of the session, we would meet at a resort to tell stories about our victories, evaluate our performance, and plan for the coming year.

Other times simple rituals revived people's energy. One woman talked about her version of downtime: "Sometimes it's just coming home and sitting on the couch with my dog. But I can tell the difference when I don't do this. I feel a whole lot better when I do." Another person takes breaks during the workday:

> I punctuate the day by either walking around the street, walking through a museum, or going to a bookstore. Just something different and outside of thinking about work.

In other words, you reconnect to some other things that are important to you. I think you have to say every day, 'Who else am I?' We don't have time to contemplate any more, so we have to make time to do it.

> **TIP TWO**
>
> You may have more healthy habits than you realize. Look at some of your habits that you don't think of as healthy ritu-als. Maybe some of them are relaxing or rejuvenating for you. If someone finds dusting rejuvenating, anything's possible.

Getting Enough Sleep

A number of people addressed the importance of getting enough sleep. One woman said, "If I can get seven hours of sleep, I'm golden." Another person talked about consistent amounts of sleep: "I tend to go to bed and get up at the same time almost every day within an hour or two of the same time. My typical pattern is to go to bed around 10:30 p.m. and get up about 6 a.m. I do that day in and day out. That way I can make sure that I consistently get enough sleep."

> **TIP THREE**
>
> Get enough sleep. Most people indicated that they needed at least seven hours of sleep regularly to feel their best. Set up a routine of going to bed and getting up in the morning at regular times.

Breathing Is a Healthy Ritual

The habit of breathing deeply is one of the most basic and important healthy rituals. But when people are under a lot of stress, they often don't use it. Shallow, fast breathing is a typical response to fear or stress. Unfortunately, that's one of the worst things you can do to your body if you are trying to stay calm. Breathing techniques work because they modulate the heart rhythm pattern, according to experts. When respiration and heart rate oscillate at the same frequency, it signals the brain to produce feelings of security and well-being.[1] There are many variations on healthy breathing techniques, but the common elements are the following:

- Breathe slowing. (Four to five seconds to inhale and four to five seconds to exhale.)

- Breathe in deeply. (Pull the air all the way down into your diaphragm.)

- Exhale completely. (Push the air out of your diaphragm and lungs.)

- Visualize while breathing. (Focus on a color, sound, phrase, smell, or the beating of your heart.)

- Repetition. (At least ten breaths are usually the minimum recommended to produce a calming effect.)

Many of the people we interviewed used some type of regular calming rituals such as meditation, prayer, or yoga. All of these activities involve breathing techniques. Others didn't do any of these more organized activities, but did stop frequently during the day to "breath deeply" to calm themselves down.

---

[1] Bruce Cryer, Rollin McCarty, and Doc Childre, "Pull the Plug on Stress," *Harvard Business Review* (July 2003), 104.

> **TIP FOUR**
>
> Build slow, deep breathing into your daily rituals. It is one of the simplest and quickest ways to stay calm when you are under stress.

Taking Time Off

Many interviewees stressed the importance of taking time off from work and getting away from your usual environment. Craig Park, a senior executive in the building industry, said he tries to go away for a week once a quarter:

> I go to places where I don't have a connection to voice or e-mail. I specifically pick places where I can slow down—not Paris or London to see every museum, but to quiet settings that are relaxing. I put those weeks on my calendar at least six months in advance, and they are sacrosanct. When someone wants to schedule a meeting that week, I tell them no, I am going to be gone. I only leave a number where people can call me in case of an absolute emergency—like if my house burns down.

Nancy Granese, a senior government affairs specialist, said, "I just leave. I go to places where no one speaks English. I go as far away from Washington as I can get, both intellectually and emotionally."

A corporate executive who also emphasized the importance of going away to relax said he spent an hour a day answering e-mail during his last vacation. This was a new behavior for him. Normally when he goes on vacation, he's completely out of touch with the office. Checking e-mail actually reduced his stress level because he wasn't sitting around thinking about the

500 e-mails waiting when he got home. Not working on week-ends was the key to another person's approach during a particularly high-pressure period of his career: "The weekdays could be hellacious—sixty hours a week for months at a time. But during that entire three-year period, I only went to the office twice on weekends."

TIP FIVE	Take time off and get away from your usual environment. Slow down. A change of "intellectual and emotional" scenery helps rejuvenate you better than staying in familiar surroundings. Checking e-mail is optional.

Pacing Yourself Is an Essential Daily Ritual

According to Jamie Gregory, senior congressional lobbyist for the National Association of Realtors, pacing yourself is important:

> Take breaks when you can, even if it is as simple as grabbing lunch with several people on a Friday and decompressing. Find an even pace and keep to it. I learned that while bartending in college. No matter how busy the place was, there was a certain speed where you were most effective. When you tried to push beyond that, you started breaking things and spilling drinks. It translates into being frenetic and is not necessarily productive.

Pushing as hard and as fast as you can for long periods of time is dangerous. You likely will produce lower quality work and burn yourself out. In an excellent book on developing healthy habits called *The Corporate Athlete*, author Jack Groppel described the importance of oscillating between energy expenditure and energy recovery.[2] The human body is designed to function well by oscillating between activities that require a burst of energy output and activities that allow energy recovery. Taking frequent short breaks during the workday to walk around, drink a glass of water, or do a quick breathing exercise helps sustain your ability to keep going without burning out. Building frequent and regular recovery rituals into your daily life is the key to maintaining your energy and staying healthy. Julie Freeman, president of the International Association of Business Communicators, mentioned an article she read in the *Wall Street Journal* that described the mistake many people make:

> It talked about people who have a habit of working really, really hard and then going off to a spa for a week. They do this over and over. It's sort of the psychological equivalent of binge and purge. The point of the article is that this is not a healthy way to balance your work and relaxation time. What we really need to do is manage our daily and weekly routine so that there is some relaxation time built in regularly.

TIP SIX	Pace yourself. Instead of pushing hard and fast all day, take energy recovery breaks regularly and frequently during the day. Your energy will last longer, you will produce better quality work, and you will be less likely to burn out.

[2] Jack Groppel, *The Corporate Athlete: How to Achieve Maximal Performance in Business and Life* (New York: John Wiley and Sons, 2000), 28.

The Trap We Can All Fall into
If We Aren't Careful

Sandra Boot, manager of a data center service bureau, described how she learned the hard way to pace herself:

> It was so easy to work an extra hour or two. The next thing I knew I was working ten-hour days. Then I was working twelve-hour days. Then I started bringing work home and going into the office on weekends. I would tell myself I would just go in for a couple hours, but ended up being there all day Saturday. My husband noticed. I didn't want anything to happen to my marriage, so I worked at getting things back in balance. I put a box around the hours I worked so I had to figure out how to get the work done within that box. I started playing golf, listening to music, and being with my husband.

During that time her mother, who lived on the other side of the country, died suddenly, and it came as quite a shock to Sandra: "We were a very, very close family even though I didn't go back to visit more than a couple of weeks a year. But when she died, I thought to myself, 'I can't believe I put my job before my family.' And I promised myself that I will never do that again."

TIP SEVEN	Don't fall into the trap of working more and more until you've made your job more important than your family. Healthy rituals help you keep the balance that everyone struggles to maintain in their lives.

CHECKLIST OF YOUR HEALTHY RITUALS

What do you do on a regular basis to relax and unwind? What do you do to rejuvenate or re-energize yourself? Here is a list of possible activities from the interviewees that may be on your list, or that you want to add to your current healthy rituals:

❑ Sports

❑ Sit on the couch with your dog

❑ Exercise

❑ Hang out with friends

❑ Go for a walk or hike

❑ Hobbies like beer making

❑ Garden

❑ Play a musical instrument

❑ Read

❑ Take a break for chocolate

❑ Watch TV

❑ Go to a museum

❑ Meditate or pray

❑ Cook

❑ Eat dinner with your family

❑ Ride your bike to church

❑ Go to a cabin in the woods

❑ Do volunteer work

❑ Sing in the car

❑ Celebrate successes

❑ Call or e-mail a friend

Other activities that you do regularly to relax or rejuvenate?

_____

_____

Do you get enough sleep regularly? (For most people, that is at least seven hours.)

_____

_____

Do you take time off from work regularly?

_____

_____

Do you pace yourself during the day with frequent quick breaks for energy recovery?

_____

_____

Examples of activities for quick breaks at work:

- ❑ Drink a glass of water
- ❑ Do a few breathing exercises
- ❑ Walk around the office
- ❑ Call a friend
- ❑ Do mindless paperwork
- ❑ Eat an apple
- ❑ Meditate or pray
- ❑ Listen to music

Get Organized

"Don't touch my stacks and piles!" If you think this chapter is about time management techniques and tips for cleaning your office, you're in for a surprise. That's not what we heard during our interviews. The neatness and organizational habits of these people ranged from self-confessed neat freaks to slobs. "I'm a very organized person," said Jeff Jernigan, a banker. "But the chief lending officer of our bank is totally opposite. Man, you walk into his office, and it looks like a tornado hit it."

Not only was there a wide variety of habits, but it was clear that very few people were interested in changing their basic approach. Some wanted to make small changes or improvements in their organizing habits, but no one desired a whole new approach. For example, two people had remarkably contrasting views. Leslie Loughmiller, university professor, described her approach this way: "I have this personality of being really organized. I have to sit down and organize what I'm going to do today. I have to constantly stick to that. If I start venturing out and thinking about all the things my brain is telling me to do, I get overwhelmed and start burning out."

Another person we interviewed told a very different story. Steve Hill is president of Linux Clusters, a successful start-up company that produces and sells massively parallel supercomputers. "I look at each day as an adventure with possibilities that you just can't imagine the night before. To me, looking at a calendar that's full of appointments far into the future is my idea of hell."

One couple interviewed related a funny story about the husband's failed campaign to reform his "messy" wife. She is a Washington, D.C., attorney who was the first woman to hold various responsible tax policy positions and built a successful career using the "stacks and piles" method of organizing. She could produce the right piece of paper almost instantaneously when called upon, despite the apparent chaos. The couple married in midlife. He is an executive who was very linear and the consummate "a place for everything and everything in its place" person. Her chaos (she also confessed to smaller stacks at home) was very stressful for him. He tried to "reform" her by demonstrating how to be linear and do things the right way with the "neat desk" mode. She lost ground. She couldn't be as systematic as he was and lost much of her skill at producing the right thing from the right stack. After she adopted some of his methods, her output remained fairly consistent; however, it often took significantly more energy to accomplish her goals. They discovered that neither had the "right" way of doing things.

TIP ONE	It's probably a mistake to try to reform yourself (or your spouse). There are various ways of organizing, and one isn't better than the others. Work on making your approach as effective as possible. That's a better use of your time and energy.

If Getting Organized Doesn't Mean Cleaning Off Your Desk, What Does It Mean?

From what people told us, burnout is probably a response to the complexity of our lives and the world around us in this uncertain era. Our interviewees did not want to change their organization methods, but they expressed a great need to simplify their lives. Avoiding burnout and getting organized is not really a matter of cleaning the desk, assigning the "1, 2, 3" priorities, and using a cookie-cutter model. Rather, it's a process of identifying strategies for dealing with complexity. We've identified four dimensions for developing such strategies; you might have others. The dimensions revealed in our interviews were self-knowledge, relationships with others, use of time, and technology. Self-knowledge and relationships involve a person's mind and heart, while time and technology are the pragmatic, practical issues more often associated with getting organized.

Avoiding burnout and getting organized is not really a matter of cleaning the desk, assigning the "1, 2, 3" priorities, and using a cookie-cutter model. Rather, it's a process of identifying strategies for dealing with complexity. We've identified four dimensions for developing such strategies; you might have others. The dimensions revealed in our interviews were self-knowledge, relationships with others, use of time, and technology. Self-knowledge and relationships involve a person's mind and heart, while time and technology are the pragmatic, practical issues more often associated with getting organized.

TIP TWO	Whether you are a list maker or a "stacks and piles" builder, you need to find ways of dealing with the complexity of your life. Finding ways to simplify your life is the entire point of getting organized.

Self-knowledge: The Key to Coping with Complexity

"Know thyself"—this ancient directive has relevance today. Discovering your best organization method requires that you know who you are: your values, interests, abilities, talents, skills, attributes, motivations and drives, and strengths and weaknesses. When you know yourself, you're more likely to be realistic about your future and the project at hand. You know what you can do and where you want to go. You also can be more effective at calling on your strengths and lessening the impact of your weaknesses. Vickie J. Jones, an insurance accounting operations manager, said, "We each have different priorities in life, and it's a personal decision on how we set them and allow them to control our lives."

TIP THREE	Size up your skills, values, and interests. The priorities you set will be very personal. Work on maximizing your strengths instead of following someone else's cookie-cutter approach to organization.

Part of knowing yourself is having realistic expectations, particularly in difficult transitions to new jobs, environments, and cultures. One of the interviewees was the right-hand man for Dick Cheney throughout much of Cheney's career in government and industry. He told us the story of his transition from working in his native Casper, Wyoming, as Cheney's campaign director to running newly elected Congressman Cheney's office in the rough-and-tumble U.S. House of Representatives. He began with introductory advice: "Don't be afraid to ask questions, it isn't embarrassing. You may ask a stupid question, but you must remember the answer. Don't use energy trying to conceal what you don't know. It takes too much emotional energy."

> We were all novices, all green staff. We had all been involved in the campaign in Wyoming, so we were all insecure in Washington. We had no systems. The Capitol Hill culture was new to us. After three months of struggling, I found myself silently screaming, "I can't do it!" The staff fought constantly. In desperation, I found that the House of Representatives had a course for us new guys, and I took it. Upfront at the beginning of the course, they told us that when you go to work in a new environment with new ways of doing things and lots of new people, the first six months present a terrible learning curve. Suddenly I had new clarity. It was like crossing the desert and finding a drink of water. "It's not me. I am adequate. This is how the world works."

TIP FOUR

When you're going through a major life transition, it's particularly important to have realistic expectations of the new situation and an accurate understanding of your abilities. Ask for help and get an outside perspective to be sure you're seeing things accurately.

Knowing yourself includes taking charge of your life. This was true for a significant number of our interviewees. Jim Lunsford, training and recruitment director for Wayne Brothers, Inc. said, "The first thing is to take charge of your own life, but understand that things are going to happen that you can't control. But you can always control your reaction to it and the decision that the event causes you to make." Joe Galuszka, a cancer survivor, emphasized personal life forces in the story of his cancer struggle:

> Completely mobilize and take action. Life is too short not to be completely in the game or engaged. The most important thing I did was to engage completely in the activities and responsibilities of my life. Each day I determined those actions and put them into practice. I had to stay focused on my goals and take actions that ensured a successful outcome.

Relationships with Others: When Everyone Wants a Piece of You

Everyone must strike a balance between work and family life. We need to organize our work and family activities to keep our perspective and sustain family and personal relationships. Linda Goold, a lawyer, told us about a volunteer leader of her church who is also CEO of a Fortune 500 company and places a high value on his religious and family life. He plans his work life around his family's needs. At the beginning of each school year, this CEO, his wife, and eight children create a master calendar showing everything that each family member will be involved in during the year. This includes athletics, ballet and music recitals, church assignments, and at least one date a month with his wife. Once the family calendar is set, he takes the master calendar to work and organizes his business travel around the family's needs. Over several years as a CEO, he has missed few family events.

Even when you know where you're going, have set priorities, and planned how to get there, conflicts are inevitable. Glen Goold, a manager in Ernst & Young's National Tax Office, father of four children, and a volunteer at his church, knows that someone always wants a piece of him. He has found a workable solution to conflicts:

> I feel the most frustration when I have multiple responsibilities that are all up in the air at the same time. The way I deal with it is to look at conflicts at the priority level—which one is truly the most important *right now*? I communicate with my work associates, my family, or my church associates and let them know that I have an assignment at work (or with my family or at church) that I really need to take care of. I talk it through with the affected people and make sure that everyone understands my plan. They understand why I am doing what I am doing, and they appreciate my dilemma when I say, "Right now this commitment needs to be taken care of before I can handle that commitment."

TIP FIVE	Someone always wants a piece of us. Plan your family and friends into your life. Sometimes this means figuring out who needs you the most now and then making sure the affected people understand why you're making the choices.

Time: The Common Enemy

We all try to use time the best way we can. Our behavior is based on how our brains are wired, our own experiences, and how we process information. Even though most people interviewed were trying to use their time well, they couldn't always get it together. They had days when they couldn't quite find anything and didn't have a to-do list or the right supplies. In general, their advice was to keep trying and use whatever works best for you. Try new tools and techniques occasionally and incorporate them into your organizational strategies when they work. Don't procrastinate. As one person put it, "Procrastination is the thief of success."

Norman La Barge is a retired reserve U.S. Army Special Forces colonel. Much of his professional career was spent at Thiokol, an aerospace company in the standards lab, which was responsible for identifying and solving the O-ring problem that destroyed the *Challenger* space shuttle in the 1980s. Norm couldn't have participated in this project without the skills learned in education and training. His time challenge was attaining that education. Norm didn't start college until he was already working, participating in Special Forces activities, and married with small children. Earning a college degree was a major goal that he and his family had set together, but finding the time to study was challenging:

> Obviously, you can't succeed in college if you don't do your homework, but you can order that work so that the time you spend studying is quality time. I got myself a little tape recorder and dictated the stuff that I wanted to memorize. Driving to work and school took up about two or three hours every weekday. I used that

drive time to listen to my dictated recordings of things I wanted to memorize.

Identifying and using this "found" time allows you to perform small daily tasks that contribute to accomplishing your personal and professional goals.

TIP SIX	Give yourself credit for *trying* to use your time well. Keep looking for new ideas to add to your basic approach for staying organized. Don't procrastinate—that's the biggest time waster of all.

Whose Monkey Is This?

When you're burdened with too much, you must track which tasks and problems are your responsibility and which ones aren't. The last thing you need is a lot of distractions and energy-sucking surprises. One interviewee learned a useful habit for identifying what he needs to let go. He asks himself, "Is this *my* monkey?" If the answer is no, he happily moves on by saying to himself, "It's not my monkey." He noted that when you get the problem off your mind, you can use "your energy to do what you're good at and to not do what you're *not* good at."

TIP SEVEN	Watch out for distractions and energy-sucking surprises that aren't your responsibility. Ask yourself if this is "your monkey." If it's not, let it go and move on to things that are your responsibility.

Too Many Irons in the Fire

Despite your best efforts, you'll inevitably have the occasional meltdown or too many irons in the fire. Linda Carlisle, a partner at the White & Case law firm, said that's "when you stop completely and ask yourself, 'How am I going to survive?'" A complete stop enables you to take a literal and figurative deep breath, make a quick survey of the situation, and tackle it in small chunks. The *complete* stop is critical.

TIP EIGHT	When things get tough and you're starting a meltdown, stop and take a minute to catch your breath. Ask yourself, "How am I going to survive?" Take a look at what's happening, be clear about your priorities, and decide on your next steps. This helps you recover.

Technology: Taming the Beast

Our interviewees use everything from low-tech spiral-ring notebooks to high-tech software, personal digital assistants (PDAs) to assist their organizational efforts and keep track of things. However, they had a warning about high- and low-tech organizing tools—getting carried away with any tool is counterproductive.

The Palm Pilot vs. the Spiral-Ring Notebook

We heard a wide range of stories about how people use technology to help them get organized. It's similar to the clean desk vs.

the stacks and piles debate. Some people prefer high-tech solutions, while others stick to the low-tech methods as much as possible.

Bridget Brandt, marketing director of a credit union, loves her Palm:

> It has changed my life.... The first thing I do is make a list of what my goals are for the day. The last thing I do is review that list and check off the things that I have done. If there's anything I need to do tomorrow, I put it in my Palm at that time. It gives me that great feeling of accomplishment. I usually have ten to twelve things on my list for the day. I usually get to eight to ten of them. It seems like there is always something left that I wasn't able to get to. My Palm gives me a chance to go and check all those little things, and it's a great feeling to get to check all those little boxes. Look what I've accomplished today.

Two other individuals we interviewed had a different opinion of technology. According to Linda Carlisle, she is "a dinosaur when it comes to technology" and found that when she has depended on it, there were serious consequences. "I had a PDA that contained my phonebook. It blew up." Pat Vinkenes, for many years a staff tax policy expert on the U.S. House of Representative's Ways & Means Committee and now a top-level civil servant at the Social Security Administration, reminded us that everything grinds to a halt whenever something like the computer server goes down. "When it does and I have depended on it, I can't do my work."

Both Linda and Pat prefer low-tech alternatives. For more than twenty years, Linda has used spiral notebooks. She pointed to a bookshelf during our interview where there were stacks of them. She uses them to date and log what has happened. Linda also outlines the things she has to do, using that as the beginning of planning, before thinking of details and how to get from A to Z. Pat uses a blotter calendar that sits on her desk. "If it's on my calendar, I can carry it around in my head."

TIP NINE

Go high tech or low tech—whatever works for you. Do what fits your basic organizing approach and keep an open mind about trying new options. Just because the guy sitting next to you at a meeting loves his Blackberry doesn't mean you're wrong to prefer your spiral-ring notebook.

Find Somewhere to "Dump" Your Ideas

Everyone needs places to download ideas and mental lists. Most people interviewed use to-do lists as a primary tool and technology to help with these lists. Jamie Gregory, a lobbyist for the National Association of Realtors, blends technologies. Day or night, he uses a Blackberry to e-mail himself notes about what needs to be done. "Even if I'm at home and I think of something, I'll send myself an e-mail with my Blackberry, with the subject line in capitals saying TO DO." However, technology stops at a certain point. At the office the next morning, Jamie transfers the e-mail to a legal pad and keeps a running list that he checks off as items are completed. The legal pad is the central depository for what needs to be done. He thought a zealous organizational planner would tell him that isn't the best way to do things. Jamie said, "But it works for me." That's the point.

Some people used technology for their family activities. Husband and wife Brad and Jennifer Birkenholtz, finance professionals, noted the value of evaluating progress while implementing a plan. "We've got notepads . . . on computer spreadsheets. Being two finance majors, we've got the numbers crunched on Excel anyway. We can see where we're at compared to where we say we're going to be."

One person uses templates. On one project, his employer, a large membership organization, assigned him to develop workshops for community-level volunteers and potential partner organizations. It was a complex project in which he trained staff and volunteers who then led the community workshops. According to him, one breakthrough for the project was after he created a template for workshop development into which he dumped ideas. He didn't worry about where the ideas were. The template provided a framework that freed him to concentrate on the project's creative aspects.

| TIP TEN | You need to "dump" your ideas somewhere. Use your PDA, manual to-do lists, electronic templates, or any other method that fits your basic organizing approach. Don't rely on memory. There's just too much to remember and keeping it all in your head contributes to burnout. |

PART THREE

Connections and Relationships

"Friendship improves happiness and abates misery, by the doubling of joy and the dividing of our grief."
—*Cicero*

People with strong connections to others don't burn out as easily. If you create a map of the relationships in your life by drawing lines between yourself and everyone with whom you have a "good" relationship, how many lines would be on your chart? The more lines you draw, the more resources you have available to avoid burning out.

> The companies I have worked for have been so much more compelling when I've had friends there—when you care about each other more than just, "Hey, how are you doing?" It doesn't always have to be a personal friendship, but there's got to be a connection.
> — *Gene Raphaelian, management consultant*

> It's a network, and I think that's important. It's both give and take. You can't just take. Look for opportunities to be supportive, whether it's giving a person information or passing his or her name to someone that can help. Be a connector. It really pays back in having people there for

you during times of stress in ways that you might not anticipate.

— *Craig Park, a senior executive in the building industry*

Good relationships come in many forms. These can be the intimate, high-trust relationships with a spouse or best friend. They also can be the joking, friendly contact you have every day with the cashier at the cafeteria in your office building. Every genuine connection you have with another person on a habitual basis is burnout protection. This is one reason why changing jobs, moving to a new city, or a massive reorganization in your company causes extra stress. You lose many of your connections.

The flip side of good relationships is the toxic connections. These are people with whom you have regular contact who don't support or rejuvenate you. You walk away drained, irritated, or depressed. If you added red lines on your map for these people, how much red would you see? Toxic people work against you in your efforts to prevent burnout.

Build a Network of Strong Relationships

Good relationships help keep you from burning out. It's important to have people around you that you trust. Everyone we interviewed agreed with these two statements. There was less agreement about what types of relationships are helpful or what kind of help people wanted from those around them. Almost everyone commented on the importance of a supportive family and friends, but there were differences of opinion and experiences regarding the role of work colleagues.

Value of Friends at Work

Several organizations that are working to improve their employee retention rates discovered a surprising statistic. People who reported that they have a best friend at work had substantially higher retention rates. When asked to explain this correlation, the researchers said that friends provide greater personal support, which helps keep the employee from burning out.

One woman interviewed has been living with the stress of an unemployed alcoholic spouse, and she talked about the support she gets from her secretary:

> Fortunately, my secretary is also a good friend and a confidante. She is someone I trust tremendously, so I keep her in the loop on a lot of things. I told her, "If I ever just go over the edge and lose it and I can't speak for myself, when you have to put me in the mental hospital, please explain to people what's been going on in my life and why it happened." She and I just laugh about it. She keeps telling me that the fact I can acknowledge it and laugh about it probably means I won't fall apart.

The old adage "Leave your personal life at the door" may not make much sense if we are looking for ways to avoid burnout. Life is personal. Lives are not compartmentalized into separate boxes for work and home life. Most people fare better if some friends are connected to their entire life, not just one aspect of it.

TIP ONE	Having some good friends at work helps you keep from burning out.

Downside of Friends at Work

"Friends at work are great unless you supervise them. I've seen people get badly burned by that situation." This is one of the biggest drawbacks of having friends at work. Maybe you didn't start out as a supervisor or subordinate, but then one of you was promoted. Many people maintain friendships under these circumstances. A number of our interviewees believed that the value of having friends is worth the risks of this situation. However, they acknowledged that it is a potential source of trouble. Unrealistic expectations and accusations of favoritism are the most common dangers. The people who made this situation work managed to keep the friendship and the reporting relationship open for discussion. There was no pretense that this was only a personal friendship or a reporting relationship. It was both simultaneously, and there were decisions and actions regularly required in both roles. The classic advice on this issue would be to find your friends elsewhere—do not mix friendship and supervisory relationships. However, from what we heard in our interviews, the reality of people's lives often doesn't match this classic advice. There was a lot of overlap, and in many cases they made it work. Cheryl Jernigan, a former executive in nonprofit organizations, described her view of friends at work:

> Friends at work help you get through stressful times. I often would tell myself when I started at a new organization that I shouldn't form good friendships at work, but then I would find myself forming new friendships. Yeah, you're going to get disappointed at times, but I finally decided I'd much rather work in a situation where I care about people with whom I work. The bond people have with each other often is what helps them get through the difficult times.

<table>
<tr><td>**TIP TWO**</td><td>Be realistic about the downside of friendships at work, particularly in a supervisor/subordinate situation. If you are going to have a friend under this circumstance, talk openly with the friend about how you're handling the decisions and actions that go with both roles. Don't pretend it is just a friendship.</td></tr>
</table>

People in senior leadership roles, particularly the CEOs we interviewed, often thought that they were particularly restricted in having friends at work. One CEO worded it this way:

> I think this is tricky for CEOs or senior managers. I don't really feel that I have friends at work, and I do that consciously. I try to be friendly with people and have personal conversations about things like kids or puppies. It's not that everything I talk about with people at work is all business. But unfortunately, I don't think I can go out after work to have beers with people. That's why professional associations are important. You can find people with the same kinds of experiences. You can be more relaxed and discuss problems and issues in a way that I cannot always do with people at work.

<table>
<tr><td>**TIP THREE**</td><td>If you are a CEO or senior manager, it probably is better to find friends outside your organization. The higher you go in the organization, the more dangerous mixing friendships and work relationships becomes.</td></tr>
</table>

Loyalties Keep People Going through the Rough Times

Relationships among people working together are often the inspiration that keeps them going under circumstances in which they would have thrown in the towel otherwise. Linda Mattson, a corporate division head, described the way she dealt with a particularly rough transition. New management was dismantling the division that she and her staff had built from scratch over an eight-year period. It was a painful time for all to live through: "As angry as some of it made me, I couldn't do anything about it, so I focused on what I could do something about. First, I took care of myself (fitness and finances) and then that allowed me to spend all my energy on what I could do, which was to help the people who worked for me get through the change. That was what was important." We heard this theme of loyalty to the troops repeated in a number of interviews.

Bob Kulbick was the CEO of a subsidiary of an insurance company when new management came in and put the company in limbo for eighteen months while it decided whether or not to sell the subsidiary, shut it down, or keep it. The management team that had worked with Bob to build the profitable business unit over the previous four years stuck with him through that frustrating time. When asked how he kept from burning out, he talked about the leadership team who stuck it out with him: "I had a support group around me that was in the same boat." He also talked about the employees who were counting on them. "We didn't want to abandon the people who would be left behind. It would be just like the ship is sinking and the captain and his support staff took the only lifeboat and left everyone else to drown. You can't do that. You couldn't live with yourself." When the subsidiary was finally sold and it looked like his team was going with the new company, one of Bob's team members came up to him and said, "Bob, I'd follow you anywhere, even if only out of morbid curiosity."

Sometimes it's the relationships that keep you going when the work itself stinks. This is just as true for the leaders as for the rest of the team. Ed Gallagher, a marketing director at a global pharmaceutical company, summed it up: "As the leader of the group, I had the responsibility for ensuring that I didn't burn out, or at least didn't look like I was burning out, because I had to keep them going. And that kept me going too."

TIP FOUR	Sometimes you weather hard times for the team when you wouldn't if you were facing the trouble alone. Focus on your loyalties to the people you work with, and often they keep you from burning out.

Using People You Trust as Resources

One person described the importance of people as resources: "Know where the resources are. You should never be in a position where you have to make a list of them. You should know who they are. Call on them. Push them out in front and you'll get credit too."

When asked what kind of help they requested from friends, the answers fell into four general categories:

- asking for advice
- changing perspective on the situation
- providing moral support and encouragement
- helping with tasks

Ina Lavin, human resources manager, Boston Communications Group, talked about her nine-month job search after being laid off from her executive-level human resources position. During this time she received a great deal of advice and moral support from her friends and colleagues: "It was really important that people I knew were rooting for me, would be there to talk with me, let me cry on their shoulder, offer me words of advice. These were people I could admit it to when I was feeling like crap. My friends were really there for me." One piece of advice she received from a friend was especially helpful:

> I was preparing to go on an interview and knew I was a finalist for this job. I was going to meet the CEO, CFO, and CTO. I was really nervous about it, so one of my friends sent me an e-mail that I had sent her in the past when she was going on an interview. She said, "Just remember what Ina Lavin said: Remember to have fun on your interview." And I wrote back to her and said, "Thank you for throwing my own words in my face, because I needed to hear that." And I did have fun at that interview.

She got the job.

Chris McEntee, a health care executive, talked about a different kind of help that is important to have from at least one trusted colleague:

> You need someone who will come to you, close the door to your office, and tell you that you really screwed up. I remember one person in particular. We worked really well together. I will never forget this one day when I made a really big mistake. He pulled me in my office and said, "Now, you know. . . . " And he told me what he thought about my mistake. At first I was really upset. But then I looked at him and said, "That's a really good point. Thanks for telling me." It is really important to have people around you who you know will tell you things like that. And the higher you go in the organization, the harder it is to find.

She also pointed out that it is essential that "you know the person has your best interest at heart. I trusted him. If it had been someone else, I might have reacted differently. We haven't worked together for years and we still talk once in a while."

TIP FIVE	Look for at least one colleague who will tell you when you're screwing up. It must be someone you trust so you will listen to the feedback.

A number of people admitted that they were better at asking for the first three types of help than they were at the fourth one—requesting help with tasks. This was true in personal and work situations. Ramona Magid, a cancer survivor, identified this as one thing she wished she had done differently when going through treatment:

> Since that time my friends have said to me, "Why didn't you let us do anything for you? We would have felt so much better if we could have helped you more." And I realized that was a mistake. All I was thinking about was keeping it together and being a mommy to my four-year-old daughter. But it's important to let people help you . . . go to doctor appointments with you or run errands for you. I was trying so hard to make sure everything was normal, and it wasn't normal. Everyone is better off if you let people help you.

TIP SIX	Ask for four types of help from friends you trust: advice, gaining perspective, encouragement, and help with tasks. The latter is the most difficult request for most people; do it anyway. Friends are often willing to help more than you let them.

How Large Is Your Network of Connections?

If you have a large informal network of relationships, it can provide a broad range of resources when you need help. This network can be made up of friends, fellow team members from past projects, internal customers and suppliers, or a rival from the lunchtime basketball game. The question isn't so much who the people are, but how large is your network of high-quality connections. If your network is small and you have lots of repetitive contact with a few colleagues, you may be in a clique, not a broad network of connections.

Barbara Glover, a salesperson for a high-tech company, talked about a time in her life when she was going through a divorce, moving, and was out of work at the same time. Not only had she lost her job, but she changed careers at that point from human resources management to sales:

> It was not a slam dunk. People were wondering why they should take a chance on a middle-aged woman who's just made a career change and really has nothing to show for it. I was lucky to have really good friends who would sit and talk with me. They came from different places. Some were work friends and others were people I had known with my ex-husband. And in a bizarre way, some of them were almost complete strangers. People I didn't really know until I was at the crisis point. One woman was my real estate agent. We just clicked and she would call me to meet her for coffee to just sit and talk for a bit.

TIP SEVEN

Build a large network of informal relationships. If each relationship was a line on a map, how big is your map? If your map is small with only a few lines, you're probably in a clique and you're too isolated. The larger the network, the less likely you will burn out.

Be a Good Friend

Make sure you give as much as you get. Look for opportunities to be supportive of other people's needs. Ray Rasmussen, an executive in the technology industry, gave an example of how a person he had helped in the past reappeared in his life just as Ray's job was ending: "Make a habit of doing the right thing, and good things happen to you. The contact for my new job came from a guy I helped get a job somewhere else and then five years later he sought me out and said, 'You're the right person for this job.' And it came just at the time I was leaving my old job."

TIP EIGHT	Having people you can turn to as resources is a two-way street. Make a habit of offering help to people. Don't keep score. It will balance out in the long run.

Listening is one of the most important skills for being a good friend, according to almost everyone who mentioned the significance of relationships. They often talked about how important it was to have friends who would listen to them when they were having a hard time. And it works the other way too. You must be a great listener—not just an adequate listener, but a *great* listener—there is a big difference. Listening is a skill that everyone can learn if they work at it.

<table>
<tr><td>TIP NINE</td><td>Ask yourself the following questions to develop the discipline of being a great listener:
Does my mind wander when they are talking?
Do I make silent judgments?
Am I thinking of what I am going to say next?
Is the person talking more than I am?</td></tr>
</table>

Several friendship behaviors were mentioned over and over by our interviewees. They often used the same words to describe these important behaviors.

<table>
<tr><td>TIP TEN</td><td>Don't damage relationships. Focus on the long-term relationship, not evening the score in the current situation:
"Don't speak ill of others. It will get back to the person."
"Don't burn bridges."
"Don't participate in gossip at work."
"Defend other people in their absence. You'll have more allies."
"Don't hold grudges."</td></tr>
</table>

One of the highest areas of agreement among the people we interviewed and surveyed was the importance of relationships in avoiding burnout. Having friends and being a good friend is often what gets you through the hard times in your life.

Defending Yourself from Toxic People

"Psychic vampires" was the term used by one interviewee to describe toxic people. They drain the energy and life out of you. There isn't one specific pattern of behavior that makes people toxic. Characteristics that are annoying and draining for one person may not bother someone else. However, there are some common themes that frequently were identified in our interviews:

- relentless pessimist

- angry critic

- controlling corrector

- whiner

- backstabber

This by no means exhausts the list of possibilities. Knowing which of these types drives you nuts is the first step in protecting yourself. For example, you may find perpetually angry people exhausting to be around, but can ignore predictions of doom and gloom from a pessimist fairly easily. Everyone has personality quirks that can be annoying at times, but that does-n't necessarily make them toxic. It's the psychic vampires that need to be identified.

<table>
<tr><td>TIP ONE</td><td>Answer the questions: Who are the toxic people in your life? Which of their behaviors wear on you? If being around certain people regularly leaves you feeling tired, depressed, or irritated, they are toxic to you.</td></tr>
</table>

First Choice: Eliminate Toxic People

The easiest solution works well, but isn't always possible. If you identify someone who is toxic for you, stop spending time around that person. This sounds obvious, but people don't always do it even when it's quite possible. Inertia keeps people's habits in place. In this case the entrenched habit is spending time around toxic people when you could easily avoid doing so.

In a work setting, avoiding some people can be difficult. One person who worked with large numbers of volunteers talked about having to deal with the ones who were toxic.

> Some of the volunteers were there because they saw an opportunity to aggrandize themselves, but they didn't really want to do any work. They were toxic because they were unproductive and thought everyone else on the team should do their work, so I developed strate-gies for isolating these people and even getting rid of them. Sometimes I would try to counsel them quietly.

In the most extreme cases, I simply didn't invite them to the informal meetings and events where the real work got done. My most effective tactic was to have group planning meetings and talk about how difficult the work was going to be. I would tell the group, "If you don't want to do it, then you probably ought to resign from the committee now." It often worked. They quit.

A woman who survived cancer remembered that one of the most common and helpful pieces of advice she received from friends after her diagnosis was to avoid spending time around toxic people: "Under most circumstances, these people are annoying to be around and can contribute to burnout, but if you are fighting for your life, they are downright dangerous to your health. Stay away from them."

TIP TWO	The easiest strategy for dealing with toxic people is to avoid being around them. It isn't always possible, of course. However, before you try the other strategies, ask yourself if you really must keep them in your life.

Second Choice: Limit Your Contact

Many people told us that the problem with eliminating toxic people from your life is that it isn't always possible. What if the toxic person is your boss, a project team member, or your brother-in-law? Most individuals don't want to quit their job or abandon their family to avoid the toxic people. If some people are toxic but you can't or don't want to eliminate them from your life, the second easiest strategy is to limit contact with them. Don't invite them to your house as frequently, don't sit with them at lunch so often, and don't say "yes" every time they ask you to do something with them. When you have conversations, keep them shorter than you would with nontoxic people. Discuss necessary work issues politely but efficiently and then move on as quickly as possible. Be prepared to use conversation closers such as, "Thanks, that was useful information. I'll get back to you on that." Then walk away or hang up. If you opt for the "limiting contact" strategy, avoid the temptation of being drawn into an argument or debate, especially if it is about the behavior you find toxic. For example, trying to talk a pessimist into being optimistic about the topic you're discussing is hopeless. You will fail and walk away feeling drained from the effort.

One interviewee described her efforts to avoid a toxic colleague:

> It drove me crazy to work with her on a project. She was overly cautious, negative, and distrusting about everyone's ideas. She slowed decision making down to a crawl. We worked in a fast-paced entrepreneurial company where everything was due yesterday. Trying to stay on schedule with her in the picture was exhausting. Once I tried to talk her into seeing it the way the rest of the team did. That was a mistake. She ended up yelling at me, so I learned to avoid her as much as I could. I tried to stay away from projects that involved her. And when I was stuck working with her, I did as much work as I could outside the meetings.

Lots of us took that approach. That way by the time we got to the meeting, all her nay-saying was too late. The work was already done. She didn't like any of us, but frankly we didn't care. We just ignored her as much as we could. I really liked that job, but when I left a few years later, one of the best parts of leaving was that I never had to see or talk to her again.

TIP THREE	If you can't eliminate some toxic people from your life, limit contact in every way you can. Avoid being drawn into protracted conversations with them. The last thing you want to do is try to persuade them to change their ways. Save your energy and move on as quickly as possible.

Third Choice: Confront the Toxic Person

Confronting people about their behavior is the most complicated thing to do and wasn't a popular choice with most people we interviewed. "Takes too much energy and probably won't work anyway. It's better to avoid them or learn to ignore them," said one interviewee. However, there was one case in which someone suggested that confrontation was worth the effort—when you're setting limits with the toxic person. This woman described a situation with a cousin whom she often saw at family events. "He says bad things about me and just sucks my energy. For example, when I see him, he tells me I look fat. 'Man, your hips are getting large' or 'Your hair needs cutting.'

Every single time I see him, there is always something negative
he says. For a while I tried not to pay attention to it. He claimed
he was trying to help me." Finally she decided to confront him:

> I came out and said, "Look, from now on every time
> you see me, don't say anything mean to me. Because if
> you keep it up, I am just not going to be around you
> anymore." Then I had to keep reminding him. Next
> time I saw him, he did it again. I said, "That's exactly
> what I'm talking about. I can't be around that." And he
> was so sorry. You have to be patient with people
> because it's hard for them to break those habits. But
> you don't have to let them do it to you.

TIP FOUR	You can confront toxic people to set limits on their behavior with you. Unless you're a trained therapist, you won't change their personalities, so don't try. Just be clear about the specific behavior you want them to stop doing around you. Be prepared for the probability that you'll have to remind them frequently.

Surround Yourself with People Who Give Back

One person interviewed was an entrepreneur who had been
betrayed by a trusted colleague. She talked about the lessons
learned from that experience

> I had a key person, second in command, who was con-
> ning me. She misrepresented lead reports and went on

> business trips that turned out to be vacations. When
> we confiscated her laptop, we found out it was all a
> huge con. At the same time, another employee was
> diagnosed with terminal cancer. Then we lost a big
> contract because another company offered a kickback
> to get the work. I had never gotten sick during the nine
> years of starting and building this company, but I did
> then. I got pneumonia and thought I was going to die.
> I was so sick I couldn't even go to the funeral of the
> employee who died.

This experience caused her to rethink her entire approach
to the business. She described one reaction this way: "I backed
off from any social engagement in my company for about six
months until I felt I had a better balance. Since then I have
made sure to surround myself with people who can give back.
When I'm really down, they can be stronger, so I think I am
doing things smarter now." In other words, she is making more
effort to ensure that she has people around her that she can
trust and rely on for help. You may not be able to eliminate all
the toxic people from your life, but make sure you have lots of
trustworthy people around you to counterbalance the effects of
the toxic people.

Another interviewee worked with a team that was faced
with "a really ugly situation" of working closely with a politician
who treated people very badly.

> He would scream at the top of his lungs and call you
> every name in the book. If you didn't go to Harvard,
> you weren't smart enough to lick an envelope. Every
> day someone would be crying. Everyone hated to go to
> work. You were walking on eggshells, not knowing

what was going to set him off today. One thing that happened was that the staff bonded much more closely because all we had were each other. Most of us were young and from out of town, so we were each other's family away from home.

TIP FIVE

Make sure you surround yourself with people you trust and who give back. You may not be able to eliminate all the toxic people from your life, but you can ensure that you have a number of high-trust relationships that can help you weather the problems caused by toxic people.

Are You a Toxic Person?

This may be an uncomfortable question to ask yourself, but it's important that everyone stop and ask it once in a while. Most toxic people are not villains. The politician described previously who yelled at people and treated them abusively is probably either a cruel, uncaring person or seriously disturbed. However, most people aren't. They're just normal human beings who are well meaning but annoying. As one person put it, "They are people who have not learned to manage themselves very well."

Ask yourself the following questions:

- Do you often leave people feeling tired, depressed, or irritated after they have been around you?

- Do people seem to avoid being around you?

If you answer "yes" to these questions and these answers fit your experiences with many people in your life, then wake up. You're probably toxic. Do something about it. Not only are you contributing to other people's burnout, but you'll burn out too. In most cases, the only thing that is even more unhealthy than being around a toxic person is being the toxic person yourself.

> **TIP SIX**
>
> Ask yourself the following question once in awhile: Am I a toxic person? Do you regularly leave people irritated, tired, or depressed? Do people seem to be avoiding you? These are not good signs. Do something about it before you burn yourself out as well as the people around you.

TOXIC PERSON CHECKLIST

Answer the following questions to help you decide if you have toxic people in your life. If you answer yes to three or more questions about the same person, that person may be toxic to you.

Do you have the following experiences frequently with any person in your life?

Yes   No

❑   ❑   You feel exhausted after you've been with him or her.

❑   ❑   You get angry at things that he or she says or does.

❑   ❑   You want to argue about things this person says or does, but it seems pointless.

❑   ❑   You're more depressed or irritable after you spend time with this person.

❑   ❑   You make excuses when this person asks you to do something with him or her.

❑   ❑   You dread getting together with this person once you've made plans.

❑   ❑   When you are with this person, you're anxious to get away as quickly as possible.

❑   ❑   You tense up when this person comes near you.

Be a Good Team Member

" If you are not able to work with groups, it's going to be very difficult for you in your career," said a young CPA about the importance of working well on teams. "You first participate as a team member and then eventually you have an opportunity to lead teams. You have to be able to handle both roles, or you won't be successful and you may burn out."

Teams are commonplace in all forms of organizations. In fact, the team is the standard organizational unit in the workplace. Team members can be from similar or markedly different functional areas. Their leaders can be managers or peers. The team can have long- or short-term agendas. Employees often are expected to do their individual jobs and also serve on teams. At times these team assignments have nothing directly to do with each person's regular tasks.

Being a good team member or leader isn't easy. If the people serving on the team aren't skilled in their roles, the team likely will fail at its mission. Even if the team accomplishes its goals, the experiences along the way for the participants can be frustrating and waste time. Poor teamwork causes stress and burnout.

TIP ONE Much of your career success depends on your ability to be an effective team member and team leader. That's how work is accomplished today.

Three Traits of Effective Team Members and Leaders

Some of the most enthusiastic stories about teamwork came from the isolated world of law making in the U.S. Congress. The public thinks of Congress almost exclusively in terms of elected officials, but nearly all day-to-day work is done by small staffs of dedicated professionals serving at the pleasure of their elected bosses. The stories we heard weren't about partisan politics, personalities, or the pursuit of ideologies. Rather, they focused on the nuts and bolts of moving from an idea to a new law. In a word, it takes teamwork. Three attributes describing an effective team member and a strong team leader emerged from the interviews:

• Make the boss and organization look good.

• Cooperate and share the credit.

• Get along with everyone.

Make the Boss and Organization Look Good

An executive with a Fortune 100 company told us about working in the competitive world of tax legislation early in his career. His boss was Congressman Dan Rostenkowski, chairman of the powerful U.S. House of Representatives' Ways and Means Committee, which is responsible for all federal tax law and half of federal spending. The committee staff, as a team, had tremendous pressures with constant deadlines. These conditions could have burnt the staff out, but seldom did.

He described the staff members' willingness to support their goals and each other. "Whatever stress or burnout factor was involved, you didn't think about that. You thought, 'We've got a goal to make here, we've got to get together with the gang, and we've got to push this thing. If we run up against a brick wall, we're going to have to figure out how to deal with brick walls. We're in the soup together here, and we've got to solve it.'"

> **TIP TWO**
>
> Your boss and organization count on you to solve problems and produce good results. Concentrate on the positive aspects of the work. Get energized and figure out how to overcome obstacles.

Just as the team must strive to reach the goals and results its leader aspires to, the team leader must support the team and invest in it to be sure that its members perform well. Len Foster, divisional vice president for distribution at Canadian Tire Corporation, told us about the importance of a leader's role: "You need to have absolutely the best possible people working for you who share your vision and values. Commit yourself to their personal growth and provide a work environment conducive to high-quality work and fun." Len firmly believes that this prevents burnout for a team leader as well as the team members. "When you're buried, you know your team will pick up the slack."

TIP THREE | Leaders must invest in their teams by sharing the vision and values, providing training, and creating a positive and friendly work environment.

Cooperate and Share the Credit

John Sebree and Jamie Gregory are part of a team of six lobbyists at the National Association of Realtors. They believe their team is effective because they cooperate and their leader fosters trust. Jamie described the team's willingness to lend a hand:

> We try to support each other. One of us may run into a problem, and we can call for help. "John, I'm on the Hill and I need background material. Can you bring more?" Or better yet, John had paid for a luncheon where Senator Trent Lott was going to be speaking while he was still majority leader. John couldn't go, so he asked me to go. John wasn't afraid that I was stepping on his turf. He said, "Look, we need coverage at this lunch. You know the points to get across." He trusted me to go and represent not only the organization, but himself as well.

John noted the ongoing planning and coordination by team members. He described brainstorming sessions for solutions and new strategies:

> We sit around the table every Monday, first with the full Government Affairs staff. Then the lobbyists stay and work with the issue people who have bills moving that week or to brainstorm on refining our message. Then we

stay longer just to brainstorm where we go from here. We scope out the week and what we'll do. During weeks when it's really going fast, the lobbyists will have short fifteen-minute meetings every afternoon to regroup, discuss what we've come up with, and develop a new plan. We love being under the gun. Suddenly, you are spending every day figuring out how to move the ball.

Effective team leaders instill the spirit of cooperation. John and Jamie learned a great deal about cooperation from contrasting experiences with a bad team leader and an effective one:

One leader we had didn't trust us; therefore we didn't trust him. He was secretive. He never shared information and rarely even told us what his schedule was. He wanted all the credit for everything. It was not a healthy atmosphere. Our current team leader trusts us and expects us to do a good job. He gives us feedback and treats us as equals. He is a very open operator. If he doesn't communicate with you, you can go up and ask him and he is going to tell you what you need. Most importantly, he understands that if we do well, he does well. It isn't about his success; it's about our success. He knows that if the folks that report to him get the credit for doing something good, he gets the credit also.

	Teams are effective when team members cooperate, help each other, and communicate frequently. Leaders must trust their teams, and teams must trust their leaders.
TIP FOUR	

Get Along with Everyone

Personality differences among team members can contribute to burnout. Abraham Zaleznik, noted business management theorist, put it this way: "Organizations are indeed social systems, arenas for inducing cooperative behavior. And as such, they are quintessentially human and fraught with all the frailties and imperfections associated with the human condition."[1] These imperfections mean that not everyone will like all their teammates or be able to communicate well with them. However, you must figure out how to get along with each other. If your team is to accomplish its goals and keep from burning out, you can't waste time dwelling on team members' personality irritants.

During his time on the Ways and Means Committee, a staff person worked with people with more-than-adequate egos who faced tremendous pressures with constant deadlines. His advice was to ignore turf and share power with others; they'll reciprocate in kind: "I think we had a great group of people who were willing to give up a little something for the other persons on the team. A certain amount of flexibility is important, too. Because if you aren't flexible, you break. Bend a mile, but never break."

TIP FIVE	Be flexible. Learn the art of give and take and share power with each other.

Giving up a little for the benefit of everyone else is crucial to team success and can even lead to bonds that may reach well beyond the workplace. Margaret Fisher, a strategic planning

---

[1] Abraham Zaleznik, "Real Work," *Harvard Business Review* (January-February 1989), p. 60.

consultant and formerly of AARP, told us about a learning team she was a member of while seeking a master's degree in organizational behavior:

> As a learning team, we came together once a month for about four days. There was a lot of work that we did between times. We had frequent telephone and e-mail communications with each other between team meetings and had social activities that contributed to the intimate friendships we developed in supporting each other. Most of all, we helped each other succeed.

While Margaret emphasized the positive effect of cohesion and communication, Amy Turner, a human resources representative, acknowledged that sometimes people just don't get along. According to Amy, personality differences still need to be minimized if a team is to be successful:

> A lot of team members don't necessarily like each other, but teamwork requires trying to keep your personality set aside. No, you don't really like this person, but you are there for the team. You are not necessarily there for that person. You have to think of the best interest of the team. What's our goal? What are we trying to get to? That just seems to work better.

Amy also said that team members must talk though this: "We will remind each other, 'This person is very disagreeable, but we can't think about all the reasons why we don't like this person. We're on a team together, and we've got to work together and make the best of it.'"

TIP SIX	Set aside personality differences and make the best of it. Work together even when things get tough. You're there to serve the team and organization.

An effective team leader recognizes when a team is slowing down because of an inability to get along. The leader's first responsibility is to invest in the team, and part of investing is training. Team members may need training in interpersonal relations, communications, how teams operate, how to be a good team member, what roles team members play, how to handle conflict, and decision making.

Team leaders often have several roles in their organizations. They're frequently managers with line responsibilities. They may be members of management teams and team leaders for other teams; this is particularly true in flat organizations. Julie Freeman, president of the International Association of Business Communicators, described how it worked for her: "At the Dalkon Shield Claimants Trust, the organizational structure was pretty flat. There was the executive director and then each department had a manager. I was one of those managers. There were twelve of us at the same level. We didn't have any reporting relationship. We just worked together. Three or four of the other managers became very good friends of mine."

The team leader inevitably has the role of making sure the team is working efficiently and energetically. Jamie Gregory described his very engaged team leader: "He is constantly checking in with us. He will ask, 'How's everybody doing? Is everybody getting along?' We're at peak performance when I can say, 'People are busy. They don't have time to *not* get along.'"

TIP SEVEN	A prime responsibility of team leaders is energizing team members. When people are energized, they don't have time not to get along. An energized team is less likely to burn out.

Helping the Team Survive Discouraging Times

Not every leader has an optimal team working at peak performance. No leader has an optimal team working at peak performance all of the time. Ginna Gemmell, management coach, reminded us that team leaders must manage "the dark night of the innovator." Teams go through project cycles of elation/defeat, progress/no progress and optimism/pessimism. Every innovation project has its "dark night of the innovator" when it hits the bottom of the pessimism curve. A leader must recognize and manage the downside of the cycle so that the team can break through to achieve its goals. When a team hits a low point, the leader must provide a great deal of support and encouragement to help the team see the light at the end of the tunnel.

John Sebree's strategy for leaders and teammates facing this potential burnout is to develop "a *wish* to see resolution and an endpoint."

PART FOUR

Organizational Setting—Is It Helping or Hurting You?

"On the keyboard of life, always keep
one finger on the escape key."
—*Dilbert*

Organizations can be toxic or inspiring. Sometimes it is a matter of fit. Some people may be fine working in your organization, but you are uncomfortable. A hard-driving company on Wall Street, a friendly airline in Dallas, and an association devoted to protecting children probably will have very different cultures. You may fit well in one and find another toxic. And then there are the organizations that are miserable for almost everyone. Habitual disrespect, poor ethics, intimidation, or incompetence creates a Darth Vader environment that wears everyone down.

> One job was probably the closest I've come to burning out. We were a group in search of a mission, so it's real hard to see that you are making a contribution. And the guy I worked for was a nice enough guy, but he had no time management skills. He would say he was going to call me at 8 a.m., but I'd never hear from him. If he did call, it was entirely possible the "one-hour" call would go until 11 a.m. We once had a five-hour conference call. That's a huge bladder test. It was nuts.
> — *Corporate director*

I spent twenty-six years of my career not being a CEO but watching six different CEOs and everyone else I worked for. I picked up things from everyone. When I became a CEO, I finally got to use all of these ideas I've accumulated over my career. One thing I preach to the staff is, "You need to enjoy what you do . . . you spend so much of your life at work." Then what I try to do is *help* them enjoy what they do by providing them with a ton of things they can't get anywhere else. They particularly like the paid day off for Christmas shopping.
— *Jeff Jernigan, CEO of Union Bank, Kansas City*

Many interviewees mentioned times when they worked in toxic settings. In most cases people ended up leaving those situations. It may have taken some time to get out if they felt trapped, but there was general agreement that you can't live in a toxic environment permanently without being damaged.

Is Your Work Culture Burning You Out?

John was an intelligent and talented curmudgeon. He studied for but never formally entered the Jesuit priesthood. He spent much of his career in various training capacities in a large nonprofit organization. When the invitation came for the annual holiday party each year, John observed, "Ah, yes. Another opportunity for organized joy." In his opinion, the organization was full of paternalistic people who didn't like each other. Manipulation and backstabbing were the norm. For John, the "celebration" of the season was an ordeal in an organization where mediocrity was rewarded more frequently than achievement and competence. However, the phrase "organized joy" also could describe a setting where a celebration is an honest expression of goodwill among colleagues and delight in the accomplishment of the organization as a whole. Organizations can be toxic or inspiring; the ones with toxic work cultures are major contributors to burnout.

What Is a Work Culture?

A work culture is the way things really get done in an organization. Like any societal culture, a work culture has its own values, habits of behavior, ways of thinking, beliefs, and stories. You probably won't find a description of the culture in a manual or official document because much of the culture is informal and unspoken. Often people are unaware of their organization's culture. People often have no explanation when asked why things are done in a particular way in their organization. They typically respond, "I don't know. That's just the way we do things around here." However, it's important to pay attention to and understand your organization's culture. Identifying the traits of your work culture and navigating your way through them are critical to your career success.

Two types of problems can occur in work cultures that lead to a toxic situation:

- a mismatch between you and the organization's culture

- an abusive or unproductive environment that is toxic for almost all employees

Work cultures change over time because of leadership changes, mergers, reorganizations, or turnover of a substantial number of your colleagues. It can get worse or better. One interviewee described the miserable situation of working with a very difficult chairman of the board for several years. "One thing you have to remember is that this too will pass. I knew I could get through it. Fortunately, elected leaders have defined terms." Because of this time frame, he knew he wouldn't have to live with this situation indefinitely. However, sooner or later, most work settings go through substantial changes that affect your work culture. And sometimes those changes are an improvement.

TIP ONE	Pay attention to the current culture in your organization. Watch for changes. Keep asking yourself whether or not the current culture is a healthy environment for you.

Is There a Mismatch between You and Your Work Culture?

Ray Rasmussen, sales manager in a software company, described the potential mismatch.

> I think companies have personalities and reward certain behaviors, and sometimes you just don't fit. It doesn't make you a bad person, and it doesn't mean the company is a bad place either. But you have to take responsibility for understanding the personality of your company, knowing whether you are comfortable there, and thinking through your choices. I think business happens among friends. If you don't have any friends in the company, then you probably don't fit.

Whether a culture is toxic or inspiring is in the eyes of the beholder. No two people see things exactly the same way. "Organized joy" for one person may be a miserable situation for someone else.

Determine whether there is a fit or mismatch between you and your work culture. The best indicator of a good fit is your comfort level. If you're ill at ease on a regular basis with the people, attitudes, or habits of your organization, you may not fit. No matter how great the place is for other people, it can burn you out if it's a mismatch for you.

Sometimes you discover the mismatch through a disagreement about job expectations. Several people interviewed told stories about going into a company to create new positions. Everyone thought they understood and agreed on the expectations for the new jobs, but it turned out they didn't in several cases. One person described his experience of starting a new business unit in a results-driven, profit-oriented company:

> I told them when they were interviewing me that this unit was going to be expensive and not going to directly relate to sales. It was really a business development unit, so there was going to be a lot of overhead for the first four to five years. They said, "No problem. We understand." Six months later, I got called in for a tongue-lashing. "Where are your numbers? Corporate needs this stuff now." There was a disconnect. It's often easy to be blinded by the opportunity of a new job without really understanding the culture that you are coming into. Or the people hiring you do not have a clear idea of what it will take to refine the new activity you are leading. After all, they have never done it before.

The old culture is very powerful and usually doesn't change just because a new position is created and the leaders claim they want to do things differently. Over time they're likely to forget those promises and revert to old expectations.

TIP THREE	If you're starting a new function that requires the organization to do things differently, look for a potential mismatch of expectations. Six months from now the leaders may have forgotten that your job is supposed to be "different," and they're expecting you to behave and produce like everyone else in the company.

Are You Working in an Abusive or Unproductive Culture?

Abusive or unproductive work cultures make almost everyone miserable. They can take many forms, but usually involve some sort of mistreatment of individuals. One person remembered a corporation where she worked early in her career. The employees nicknamed her boss Darth Vader and referred to his black BMW as the Death Star. His most memorable trait was vindictiveness toward anyone who crossed him.

Another interviewee experienced a setting in which hoarding information was the cultural expectation. "The modus operandi was to reward people for hoarding information. The competition became not whether you did a good job, but whether you got information, hoarded it, and got to the boss first. I was very uncomfortable. It was silly and a waste of time, energy, and talent."

One individual talked about the problems that occurred when his company implemented a measurement system that "was so out of whack we were measuring all the wrong things." He recalled a situation in which a colleague was given a $10,000 cash bonus for high productivity. Co-workers knew that it was impossible to perform at the level the person claimed. He would have had to work 500 to 700 hours a month to produce those results. "We were all laughing. The boss still gave the guy the money, and everybody knew the statistics were bogus. So the next thing that happened was that everybody else started to make their statistics bogus so that the boss wouldn't fire them. People spent more time trying to cover their back-sides internally and beat the system than they did trying to do a more effective job for the clients."

An executive told a chilling story about systematic sexual harassment at an international public relations firm where she had worked. During her tenure in the organization, this woman reported to a senior executive (we'll call him Harry) who regularly made inappropriate and offensive comments to her. She developed strategies for deflecting Harry's advances and made her own peace with the relationship. She stayed in the organization because she loved her clients and thoroughly enjoyed the challenges presented in her work. However, one summer an intern broke down. The intern was working for a man (we'll call him Sam) who reported to the same senior executive. Sam called meetings with a group of the young summer interns each Monday morning for the purpose of "regaling them with the stories of his weekend sexual exploits. They were made to sit there and pretend to be amused and chuckle on cue." At that point, the executive we interviewed knew she had to address the problem. She interviewed the interns individually; all told similar stories about the meetings and volunteered other sordid information. She called in the legal and human resources departments. She then confronted Harry with the information and told him, "Unless you want me to throw Sam off the balcony right now, you better get him in here and fire him now with cause." Harry waffled. She went on, "Look. If the morality issue doesn't get you, then this will. You are making the company liable. Each of those young women can sue the company, drag us through the smut, and ruin this company if you don't act immediately." Harry gave in and fired Sam, but he never understood that his and Sam's behaviors were completely inappropriate.

TIP FOUR	Abusive or unproductive work cultures take many forms, but one common trait is mistreatment of individuals working for the company. Even if the mistreatment hasn't affected you personally, you're at risk.

What Is a Healthy Work Culture?

Many people talked about times when they had jobs they loved. They talked about how important this was in avoiding burnout. When the jobs were high pressure and stressful, they could handle it relatively well because of a pleasant or inspiring organization.

Rick Woodbury is a real estate developer who, with his family, owns several shopping centers, office buildings, and hotels. His grandfather founded the business and his father, uncle, brothers, and several of Rick's cousins have key management roles in the corporation. As Mr. Woodbury (the founder) made the transition to retirement, Rick became CEO and his brothers also expanded their roles in the business. Rick told us how he tries to make sure that the non-family members he hires fit the company's culture:

> I tell people when we hire them, "You will know fairly quickly whether or not you are going to like working here. If you don't, it's not a personal attack on me. We are a particular environment. If you don't really like this, then it is not for you." We've done really well in keeping people for the last fifteen years. We don't have very much turnover of key people. I have a hotel manager who has been with us for seventeen or eighteen years. I have another one who has been with us for twelve years. For hotel managers, that is unusual. We've grown, so they have had some other opportunities. They started at a lower position than they are now, but we tend to work with people so that they can have a meaningful career.

Rick's challenge is integrating new employees into what most people perceive as a closed family company.

> The question I ask myself is "Can we make this more of a company family rather than a family company?" I feel really strongly that the people who work here have to feel like they can relate to this atmosphere. Will they ever be president? Likely not. Likely a family member is going to be the next president. But can non-family members get responsibility? Can they get opportunity?

We can give them almost everything but the top title. They can do their own development plan and be in charge of it. They have an opportunity to learn and participate financially in our success. But the main quality that keeps them here is that they enjoy our culture. They enjoy the friendliness. We insist that they have the same value system and ethics as those of us who founded and continued the company. Those without them don't stay very long. Even though they are competent, I don't care that they leave, so I think we've avoided the toxic culture that way.

Pay Attention to Culture When You Apply for a Job

Often people pay too much attention to the job description and salary and not enough attention to the work culture when interviewing for a new job. Ginna Gemmell, founder and president of GlidePath®, Inc., told us about being recruited to work in a company early in her career:

> I felt the climate to be adversarial, even though I knew a number of the employees there. It was old home week when they saw me. Still, I felt it was too frenzied, too slapdash, a little dingy and behind the curve. The walls just spoke to me. I was offered a good position, but I didn't take it. Reading the culture before joining an organization can help us find a place to flourish and avoid a great deal of heartache.

Glen Goold, a manager in Ernst & Young's National Tax Office, pointed out that assessing the work culture can be particularly difficult for young people coming straight out of school. "They don't really know what they are getting into and they often find it was not what they expected. It is not uncommon for them to struggle as they adjust to the new culture."

TIP FIVE

Pay attention to your intuition when interviewing for a new job. Be careful if the atmosphere doesn't feel right to you. Ask current employees to tell you stories about life in the organization and meet as many people as possible. Ask them what they like about working for the company. Vague answers or answers that don't match your work preferences are warning signs.

CHECKLIST ONE: HALLMARKS OF AN INSPIRING CULTURE

How often do these practices occur in your work culture?	Most of the Time	Sometimes	Infrequently
Bosses are caring and compassionate.	❑	❑	❑
People and the organization are open to change.	❑	❑	❑
People help each other when problems arise.	❑	❑	❑
Employees are valued.	❑	❑	❑
Communications are open, enabling concerns and grievances to be known and resolved.	❑	❑	❑
Bosses manage the toxic emotions of their subordinates.	❑	❑	❑
Technical skills and knowledge as well as emotions are valued.	❑	❑	❑
Effort and resources are committed to the development of people.	❑	❑	❑
The organization promotes trust and fair play.	❑	❑	❑
Anyone is free to question the traditional ways of doing things.	❑	❑	❑

CHECKLIST TWO: INDICATORS OF A TOXIC CULTURE

Indicator	Not Applicable in My Organization	Doesn't Affect or Annoyed	I'm Unhappy or Annoyed	It Overwhelms Me
Unsustainable workloads or unrealistic expectations	☐	☐	☐	☐
Endless cost-cutting and/or downsizing	☐	☐	☐	☐
Pervasive dishonesty or lying	☐	☐	☐	☐
Rigid rules and regulations	☐	☐	☐	☐
Not talking about problems or tough issues	☐	☐	☐	☐
Pressing too hard for quick solutions	☐	☐	☐	☐
Information hoarding	☐	☐	☐	☐
Lack of vision or competing visions	☐	☐	☐	☐
Extreme competition for scarce resources	☐	☐	☐	☐
Tolerance of mediocrity or nonperformance	☐	☐	☐	☐

☐ ☐ ☐ ☐ ☐ ☐ ☐ ☐ ☐ ☐   ☐ ☐ ☐

☐ ☐ ☐ ☐ ☐ ☐ ☐ ☐ ☐ ☐   ☐ ☐ ☐

☐ ☐ ☐ ☐ ☐ ☐ ☐ ☐ ☐ ☐   ☐ ☐ ☐

☐ ☐ ☐ ☐ ☐ ☐ ☐ ☐ ☐ ☐   ☐ ☐ ☐

Sexual harassment

Racial or other discrimination

Ineffective communications

New ideas given short shrift

Warring factions with numerous accusations

People bullying others

Bosses using threats

Control freaks abound

People betray confidences

Bosses viewed as "jerks" by employees

Employees regularly express anger or pessimism

People not helping each other

People constantly gossiping

Are You Being "Held Captive" by Your Organization?

"The one thing that I've learned over time is you have to enjoy what you do. You spend most of your life at work." This common theme was expressed throughout our interviews. Make sure you enjoy your work, and it will help you avoid burnout. If you're stuck in a job that's impossible to enjoy, find another one. As one person said, "My experience has been, if you can't change it, run away. If you stay and burn out, then you've chosen to be a victim." However, others said that sometimes leaving is easier said than done. There are times when you can't leave; even if you can, it takes a few years to make the move. One of the greatest adversities people face in their working life is feeling trapped in an organization. People work harder and longer, but the old-fashioned work ethic and social contract of "work hard and you will be rewarded" seems to fade further and further into the past. It's easy to end up feeling completely depleted.

TIP ONE Your ability to avoid burnout depends on your willingness to identify bad situations and make decisions about correcting them. You must face the hard questions of when to leave, whether or not you're at fault, and when circumstances are beyond your control.

Three Types of Captivity

Approximately one-fifth of the people interviewed commented on the gut-wrenching dilemma of being trapped in a job at some point in their career. They used visceral words and phrases such as "stuck in a rut," "held hostage," "captive," "losing the battle," and "end of the world." They identified three types of captivity: financial, structural, and personality.

Financial Traps
Slipping on the Golden Handcuffs

Face it. One reason you work is the money. If you're fortunate, you also have benefits that you rely on at least as much as the money. When the money and benefits satisfy your needs and wants, moving out of a bad situation becomes difficult.

The financial golden handcuffs take many forms. There are financial obligations that don't allow you to leave your organization unless you can replace the income immediately. Prudence can dictate that you shouldn't give up a pension, stock options, 401(k) plans, and health insurance. If you're drawing a salary that couldn't be matched if you left for someplace else, the job becomes a financial ball and chain. When feeling trapped, you must decide whether to leave or stay. Two women interviewed faced just this set of choices. One stayed, one left.

Pat Vinkenes, a senior policy maker and strategic thinker with the Social Security Administration, and her husband have worked in the federal government for about twenty years. Federal workers with that tenure are under an "all-or-nothing" retirement system more rigid than the one for workers with less tenure. According to Pat, this made her "feel constrained to continue to work in government" for the twenty-five years required to qualify for full pension benefits. Like all government workers, she has the option of making lateral moves across government agencies. However, when she needed a change, she found that very few choices were available at her senior level. She had about a dozen interviews at various agencies and six to eight interviews in the private sector. In the end, Pat chose to stay where she was. She could have sought a political appointment that would have enhanced her salary and possibly her prestige. However, this involves taking a risk because of political changes after an election. Therefore, she has stayed at her professional level for a few more years and anticipates that she and her husband will stay in government until they qualify for pension benefits. At that point, as retired senior officials, they no doubt will have opportunities to work or consult in the private sector.

Another top-rated manager went in a different direction. After several years at one company, she was offered a job at a major food company. "They had me on track to go right up the ladder to vice president. They laid out my whole career." She began to feel trapped. "I took a look at the path they would put me on, and I thought, 'No, I want an interesting life, not a corporate life. The last thing I want to do is get locked into a life based on peanuts and pretzels.'" She didn't take the offer. Instead, she left her job and went out on her own as an entrepreneur and consultant. She's had ups and downs, but it's been the interesting life she sought.

	If you feel trapped in your job, decide whether to stay or leave. Evaluate the risks and benefits of both choices. Financial risks are a common reason why people decide to stay in their current jobs for awhile. If this is the case, see what you can do to improve the current job situation and plan for your future exit.

(Left margin label: TIP TWO)

Structural Traps

There's Always Been a Glass Ceiling

As the women's movement gained momentum in the 1980s and its vanguard began to achieve upward mobility in business, the phenomenon of the "glass ceiling" drew a lot of attention. The concern was that women could advance only so far. Even though they could see what was attainable at the highest levels of business, women felt they could only peer through the glass ceilings to the unreachable top rungs of the corporate ladder.

There always has been some type of a glass ceiling. The Industrial and post-Industrial ages created organizations that are pyramid hierarchies in which very few people can scale to the top. The structure of organizations demands that almost everyone tops out or reaches a plateau beyond which, despite their best efforts, they cannot climb.

TIP THREE	Just because you hit a plateau, it doesn't mean that you're past your prime or deadwood. Refuse to think like a victim. Don't waste your energy blaming others, including the organization. Be resourceful and explore your options. Getting a buyout and moving on to a more interesting job may be a possibility.

Getting Trapped in a Rut

Sometimes you get trapped in a rut in your current job. An unexpected limitation of having a high skill level is that bosses keep you at the same task year after year. You do the same thing very well over and over until boredom sets in and you feel trapped. Focusing on the skills you already have, these people don't give you the chance to expand your horizons or learn new ways of doing things.

Knowledge workers often find themselves in situations in which there's no career ladder. Their expertise is crucial to the organization's mission, but they often work alone or in teams with other knowledge workers and never enter the upward mobility ranks of management. Similarly, many managers in organizations arrive at a level at which they have only the option of staying in place or moving to another company.

Ginna Gemmell, president of GlidePath®, Inc., advised people to seek help when they get in this rut or feel trapped. "Anyone can work themselves into or out of a mental ditch. You can get out a lot faster if you don't wallow and you get help from others." Ginna followed her own advice. She faced a decision of staying with a company where she felt financially and emotionally trapped. "I worked with a great therapeutic coach until I got the courage to say goodbye to them." Other people interviewed used friends and trusted colleagues to help them figure out how to get out of a job rut.

TIP FOUR	If you feel like you're in a rut and don't like your job anymore, get some help. You can go to a professional or turn to a trusted friend or colleague for advice. It helps to have an outside perspective.

Sometimes It's Just Not the Right Fit

When Jeff Jernigan became a bank CEO, he put into practice all the good things he had seen while observing six other CEOs. He constantly tells the bank employees how important it is that they enjoy what they do. Jeff was wise enough to understand that no matter how many improvements he made, some employees wouldn't be happy at the bank. "Maybe this bank is not a fit."

Jeff believes that in those circumstances people need to move on. Regardless of the security they may have at the bank, they should leave if they hate the job. "Eventually, if people don't enjoy what they do, they really need to make that change. People hate to change, but eventually they must. It takes a lot of guts to do it because it puts you at risk. It puts you out in the open."

TIP FIVE	There's nothing wrong in admitting that you're a square peg in a round hole. If you don't like the job or organization because it's not a good fit, don't give yourself a hard time. Start working on your plans to move on to something else that you would like better.

People Traps

Working for Godzilla

A marketing executive left a position in which he reported directly to the CEO and switched to a sister company in what he understood would be a similar arrangement. However, he was misinformed and reported to the CEO through an operations zealot.

> She was one of those people that most organizations need and CEOs love. A real general. Take a directive and turn it into an action plan. But she didn't understand marketing at all. As a result, every word and image had to be approved by a committee. I knew how bad it was the day she said to me, "I don't really understand advertising. Why do we need it?" I suggested that she had probably bought things because of ads she had seen. "Never," she said. I understood completely then just how uninformed—and frankly uninterested—this person was about basic marketing practices.

For months his stomach hurt as he pulled into the parking lot each day. He went to human resources, but got no relief. Sometimes he tried charm with his boss, and other times he bit his tongue. After nine months, the company was reorganized and he no longer reported to her. It would have been a pivotal day no matter what the decision of his company would have been. "The day they made the reorganization announcement, I had another job offer in my pocket that I could have taken. It was less money, but if I had been left still reporting to that same person, I would have taken it."

How did he survive those nine months? "Every day when I left work, I would get in the car and put on music I loved. I sang at the top of my lungs all the way home." He did much more than just sing. He had to escape an impossible situation and went out and found a new job. When the reorganization came, he was prepared to leave or stay. He set some goals, looked for options, and gave himself choices.

> **TIP SIX**
>
> When you work for an awful boss, remember you have options. Set a goal to get out of the situation, and start working on it. It may take a while to find another job, but don't just sit and wait.

Please Don't Leave

Another potential trap is the opposite of having the boss from hell. In this situation, your boss values your work so much that he or she tries to talk you into staying when you've decided it's time to leave. Amy Turner, a former teacher, enjoyed her job and had the good fortune of working for a very skilled principal. When she got engaged, Amy had to decide whether to stay or move to a situation that would better suit her after marriage. "I felt trapped in that school just because the principal was so good. He tried every which way to get me to stay, so I kind of felt trapped for awhile."

> **TIP SEVEN**
>
> Sometimes you feel trapped in a job because you have a great boss who's begging you to stay. It's great to be appreciated and needed, and you'll probably reconsider leaving the job. However, you eventually must decide what's best for you.

You Can't Keep Doing Things the Same Way

If you're being held captive in a job that you don't like and feel that you must escape, you can't keep doing things the same way you've done them in the past. Develop some goals and take action in new directions. According to most interviewees, it's likely that you'll leave that job. If you stay, you must change your attitude about the job. Anne Marie Ciccone, corporate executive assistant and cancer survivor, stressed the importance of a positive outlook: "Good things usually come out of a bad situation. Although it may appear to be the end of the world, it may be the beginning of a new world for you."

"HELD CAPTIVE" CHECKLIST

Ask yourself the following questions to assess your current situation and begin setting goals and making plans to take action:

Questions to Assess Your Current Situation

1.   Am I really trapped or is it just my perception?

2.   Which of the three types of captivity am I experiencing?
     ❑   Financial
     ❑   Structural
     ❑   Personalities

3.   How much am I contributing to my problems?

4.   How much of this situation is completely beyond my control?

5.   Will this captivity be long term or short term?

6.   What is the worst thing that could happen if I stay where I am?

7.   What kind of person will I become if I stay?

Questions for Setting Goals and Taking Action

1.   What have other people done in my situation?

2.   Can I change the job situation if I stay?

3.   Can I change my attitude about the job if I stay?

4.   Can I create some new career goals and objectives to help me move on?

5.   What are the next steps to take if I consider leaving this job?

Are You Working for a Toxic Boss or an Inspiring Leader?

Most of us have lots of experience dealing with bosses and leaders. In this era of constant change, most people have had many supervisors. It's not uncommon to have had at least ten supervisors while still years away from retirement. Some interviewees worked at IBM at some point in their careers. They said there was an old "urban legend" that you average one manager for every year that you're with the company. Al Smith and Ken Gardner had thirty-year careers with IBM, and each had had more than forty managers. In addition to supervisors, everyone has been exposed to a variety of formal organizational leaders. These leaders may not be your direct managers, but they certainly affect the quality of your working life. There are also the informal leaders who play a vital role in every organization at the practical level of getting the day-to-day work done.

Toxic Bosses vs. Inspiring Leaders

Norman La Barge, who has worked in both corporate and military organizations, said, "I have had both toxic bosses and inspiring leaders, but I've found that if you have an inspiring leader, you are willing to work for them to an unusual degree without burning out." Inspirational leaders, whether formal or informal, energize people rather than burn them out. On the other hand, toxic bosses raise people's stress levels and increase the potential for burnout.

In our interviews, no one ever used the word "toxic" in combination with the word "leader." Toxic leader is an oxymoron. Toxic bosses occupy formal management positions, while inspirational leaders are found at all levels and in all types of organizations. In many cases, inspirational leaders have no formal managerial responsibilities, but still have many willing followers. If a person is toxic, no one follows him or her unless they're forced to do so by the formal organizational structure.

TIP ONE	You probably work in an organization that has inspiring leaders and toxic bosses. Whenever possible, make career choices that maximize contact with inspiring leaders and minimize contact with toxic bosses. Even if a new job description looks wonderful, working for a toxic boss will likely burn you out if you stay in that situation for too long.

How Much Do You Trust Them?

One major difference between toxic bosses and inspirational leaders is the level of trust. An interviewee talked about what he looks for in a leader:

> Trust is the key, and it has four components: truth-telling, promise-keeping, fairness, and respect for the individual. We surveyed people in the company I worked for and if a person in a leadership position, formal or informal, didn't get high scores in all four of these areas, he would have a hard time leading a change initiative because people didn't trust him enough to follow.

TIP TWO

Trust is an essential element of inspirational leadership. The four components of trust are truth-telling, promise-keeping, fairness, and respect for the individual. Use these four traits to assess your leaders' trustworthiness.

Toxic Bosses Believe in Theory X

Most toxic bosses have what Douglas McGregor has identified as Theory X assumptions.[1] Theory X describes assumptions toxic bosses make about their employees:

• Work is inherently distasteful to most people.

---

[1] Douglas McGregor, *The Human Side of Enterprise* (New York: McGraw-Hill Publishers, 1960), 33.

- Most people aren't ambitious, have little desire for responsibility, and prefer to be directed.

- Most people have little capacity for creativity in solving organizational problems.

- Motivation occurs only at the physiological and safety levels.

- Most people must be controlled closely and often coerced to achieve organizational objectives.

TIP THREE	Watch for bosses with Theory X assumptions. They're almost always toxic. They believe that people don't like to work, lack ambition, and must be directed, coerced, or controlled to achieve the organization's objectives.

Toxic Bosses Inspire Career Changes

Based on our interviews, about the only inspiration resulting from a toxic boss was the motivation to change jobs. Several interviewees were responsible for improving employee retention in their companies. They pointed out that toxic bosses were the primary reason given for leaving a job. Those individuals who talked about toxic bosses usually gave the following advice: Survive as long as you have to, but get out as quickly as you can. One person said, "My advice is to put that person in the 'Life's too short' category and move on."

One interviewee described life around her toxic boss this way:

> Our boss would cry and get hysterical and raised every-body's stress level. She conducted weekly grammar lessons for the staff. Everyone on the staff hated her. Everyone was thinking of leaving—some did. I talked to other members of the staff and found out if you were senior enough you could ignore her.

Lack of respect for their employees was a common theme of the stories people told. Leslie Loughmiller, university professor, had a toxic boss in her sixth year of teaching.

> I was teaching special education, and we had a meeting with thirteen colleagues and parents to discuss the state of the program. My supervisor belittled me in front of everyone. She told me that I was incompetent, I didn't know what I was talking about, I had no earthly idea what I was doing, and I was an ineffective teacher. I made up my mind at that point, come hell or high water, I was going to get my master's degree and get out of there. Focusing on my master's kept me from burning out.

Ginna Gemmell, a management coach, described the way some toxic managers violated the trust of people working for them:

> I have seen a few toxic bosses who were just relentless. They created anxiety, discounted their staff, and their own stress was out of control. They fired so many people and reneged on so many deals that they became menacing. They seemed to be addicted to the power rush of

their own adrenalin and the headiness of the booming '90s. They lost touch with their own humanity and began to think of themselves as invincible, above civility, and above good management principles. Only external feedback from the marketplace, shareholders, or the press can stop this kind of behavioral tsunami and create a "teachable moment" when coaching can help get to a breakthrough.

Some people we interviewed talked about the dilemma of having a job that you love and a boss who is toxic. In that case, they admitted that it might be worth waiting it out for a while to see if the situation changes. One advantage of living in a constantly changing, uncertain world is that some changes are an improvement, such as getting rid of a toxic boss.

TIP FOUR	If you have a toxic boss, start working on a plan for getting yourself out of the situation. If you love your job, you can wait out the situation in hopes that you'll get a different boss. However, in many cases, it's best to work on your options for a new job.

Inspiring Leaders Energize Their Followers

Even when times are tough in an organization, an inspiring leader can energize employees, help people maintain hope about the goals, and keep them from becoming demoralized.

James M. Kouzes and Barry Z. Posner, authors of the book on leadership called *Credibility*, described inspirational leaders as "people who make a difference and cause people to feel that they too can make a difference. Inspirational leaders set people's spirits free and enable them to become more than they thought possible."[2]

If you're working for someone like that, you know it. Maintain the relationship even when one of you moves on to other opportunities. Remember that leaders aren't limited to formal management positions. Informal leaders are present at all organizational levels. It's likely that talented informal leaders were on some of your most successful team or work projects. Pay attention to who the informal leaders are and whenever possible maintain your relationships with them throughout your career.

TIP FIVE	Maintain relationships with inspiring leaders you have known formally and informally. There are many stories of people forming strong relationships with their leaders and going on to work with them in a number of organizations.

Bonnie Barrett, director at a large pharmaceutical company, said, "I have a very supportive vice president, who leads by example. She sets clear expectations while at the same time respecting the need for balance in our lives. She manages to weave together her professional, family, and personal time. The company and my vice president support flexible work options

---

[2] James. M. Kouzes and Barry Z. Posner, *Credibility: How Leaders Gain It, Lose It, and Why People Demand It* (San Francisco: Jossey-Bass, 1993), 31.

to help balance family/school priorities with business needs." Another interviewee had a boss take him aside to encourage him to complete the U.S. Army's challenging Airborne School. This leader connected with the individual on a one-to-one basis, recognized his needs, and offered help. Sterling Colton, a retired Marriott International executive, said, "I have been fortunate to have a boss who was always supportive. I never had a situation where he was second-guessing me."

TIP SIX   Look for leaders who are good at making one-on-one contact with you. These people will be the greatest support in helping you avoid burnout.

Good leaders don't know everything. People want their leaders to be honest, competent, and inspiring. While a leader is expected to be competent, employees usually don't expect him to know their jobs better than they do. This is particularly true with professional or knowledge workers. Peter Giammalvo, Vice President, Leadership Formation, at Catholic Health East, learned this lesson when he was promoted to a new leadership position in a hospital. In the new job, he was responsible for clinical areas such as surgery and the emergency departments even though he had no medical training. Peter said, "My first meeting with the operating room nurses was pretty confrontational because they didn't see how I could understand their department when I wasn't even a nurse. Eventually, I realized that I was not hired to run those departments using a command-and-control approach. My job was to empower the people, be an effective liaison, and facilitate communication and access to the resources they needed to do their jobs. I finally figured out that you didn't have to be an expert in their area, but you have to be an expert in leadership."

TIP SEVEN	Don't expect your leaders to be the ultimate expert in your field of work. Don't require that of yourself if you're a leader. What people need most from their leaders is an effective advocate in the larger organization and support so they can put their own expertise to good use.

Learning to Lead

In some societies, people are born into leadership positions based on their bloodlines, while in other societies you can become the leader because you out-fought all challengers. There was a time when people concentrated on the physical dimensions of individuals as an indicator of leadership skill. If there was an outstanding leader who was five foot eight inches tall with thirty-one-inch arms, they looked for others with these same dimensions for leadership positions. In one large international technology company, there was a joke about this theory of leadership. It was known as the "42 Long" model because so many people in the company's management ranks wore a suit jacket that was a size 42 Long. Fortunately, current thought about leadership skills has developed beyond these old theories.

There are a number of steps you can take to develop your leadership skills. If you're interested in the intellectual approach, read any of the hundreds of books on the topic. Read biographies of successful leaders and see how they accomplished different tasks. Another way to develop your leadership skills is to find opportunities to practise. Volunteer in civic or church organizations and work into leadership positions. Take the lead in informal work groups. Learn from the leaders and toxic bosses you have known. Make a list of what actions or behaviors you liked and disliked about each leader or boss.

Conduct your own after-action reviews. The U.S. Army uses after-action reviews following every training situation to examine what went right and wrong and determine what improvements can be made. This is a high-trust-level activity because all ranks are involved in the process. Since they're training for the life-and-death conditions of combat, people know the importance of this process. Their saying is "Hard training, easy combat. Easy training, hard combat." Learning from your own successes and mistakes is one of the most effective ways to develop your leadership abilities.

TIP EIGHT

If you're interested in developing your leadership skills, read all you can about leadership, read about people who have successfully led, and put yourself in leadership opportunities. Do your own after-action reviews and learn from your successes and mistakes. Get feedback from people you trust.

TOXIC BOSS CHECKLIST

Are you a toxic boss? This is an uncomfortable question, but one that anyone in a supervisory job should ask himself or herself. Use the following checklist to determine if you're a toxic boss.

- ❏ Do I vent anger?
- ❏ Do I blame others?
- ❏ Do I have favorites?
- ❏ Do I pit people against each other?
- ❏ Do I create fear?
- ❏ Do I create resentment?
- ❏ Am I rude?
- ❏ Do I break promises?

LEADER CHECKLIST: WHAT DO WE WANT FROM LEADERS?

Use this list to assess yourself as a leader or identify the traits of leaders you work with in your organization.

- ❏ Encourages others
- ❏ Has the courage to do the right thing
- ❏ Acknowledges your work skills
- ❏ Pitches in to help during high pressure times
- ❏ Listens
- ❏ Celebrates successes
- ❏ Keeps promises
- ❏ Empowers followers
- ❏ Makes time for people
- ❏ Communicates the vision
- ❏ Promotes your advancement
- ❏ Admits mistakes
- ❏ Teaches well
- ❏ Trusts others

Conclusion

So how will you use the information in this book? When setting out to write the book, we had two purposes:

- to point out that you're much better at not burning out than you think;

- to provide practical ideas from the people we interviewed that you can add to your strategies to keep from burning out.

To help you put these ideas to use, we created one last checklist that pulls together the tips and advice. Before you put down the book, take a look at this list and add a few of these items to your current anti-burnout strategies. Don't pick too many—this added pressure doesn't help. In the future, pick up this book once in awhile, flip to the checklist again, and pick a few more items to try.

Keep in mind that one of the most consistent comments from the people we interviewed was that no one gets it right all the time. There's no perfect score on this one. Just keep working at it, bounce back as quickly as possible when life gets to you, and give yourself credit for doing as well as you do most of the time.

ANTI-BURNOUT CHECKLIST

Watch Your Thoughts

❏ Make a habit of changing your thoughts when you notice they're cynical or self-deprecating.

❏ Spend less time talking about your problems.

❏ Make up phrases or statements that help you develop the mental outlook you want and repeat them frequently during the day.

❏ If you're feeling down, keep your thoughts focused on the present.

❏ When you think about the future, paint a positive picture of a future that you want to live.

❏ Focus on any of the following categories of thoughts:

❏ Gratitude	❏ Love
❏ Optimism	❏ Courage
❏ Humor	❏ Options
❏ Spirituality	❏ Purpose/Meaning
❏ Proactivity	❏ Curiosity
❏ Altruism/Kindness	❏ Health/Energy

❏ When you're in a tough situation, take it one hour at a time.

❏ View the rough times in your life as "toughness" training. Track what you're learning for future use.

Find the Meaning

❑ Identify the meaningful elements of your work. It could be a cause, goal, or mission, or it could be elements of the work itself such as teamwork, being creative, or solving problems.

❑ Cultivate a wide range of interests in both your personal and work life. Look for ways to merge your passionate interests and work.

❑ Identify ways to add some spirit and heart to your work every day.

❑ Don't lose your curiosity, keep learning, and avoid boredom, which is the first cousin of burnout.

Get a Grip on What Really Matters

❑ Identify the "big rocks" in your life and focus on them every day.

❑ Lower expectations in some areas of your life where you wish you had the time and energy to excel but don't.

❑ Identify the "little stuff" in your life that you can let slide.

❑ Stick to your standards on an issue when you're pressured to let them go.

Keep Your Options Open

❑ Shape the game you play by generating numerous options when you're going through tough times.

❑ Ask yourself what you don't want to have happen and generate options to keep it from happening.

❑ Develop a vision for what you want your life to be.

❑ Scan for ideas continuously. Look at the world at large and inside yourself to determine what you want.

❑ Change your course if life isn't going the way you want.

Be Careful How You Tell Your Own Story

❑ Tell or write your own story and make sure you're the hero of the story, not the victim.

❑ Look for the moral of your story. What is there to learn from the story?

❑ Add funny stories to your autobiography.

Laugh More Than You Whine

❑ Use humor to keep things in perspective. "The good news is that you won't die of it. The bad news is that you won't die of it."

❑ Practise finding things to laugh about even in situations that aren't funny.

❑ Allow yourself ten-minute self-pity breaks and then get on with life.

❑ Smile more each day. Use your eyes as well as your mouth when smiling.

If You're a Control Freak, Get Over It

❏ Work on surrounding yourself with highly competent people whom you trust so you will feel comfortable delegating to them.

❏ Stop making people change the way they're doing things just because it isn't the way you do it.

❏ Cut back on "being helpful" when you know it's just a way of staying in control.

❏ To keep control freaks at bay, start using the "Don't ask permission, apologize later" approach, but be sure you don't go beyond your level and experience in the company.

Develop Healthy Rituals

❏ Make a list of your current healthy rituals. These are the habits in your life that are relaxing or rejuvenating. Keep doing them.

❏ Get more sleep.

❏ Practise deep breathing.

❏ Take more time off.

❏ Start taking short energy-recovery breaks several times a day.

Get Organized

❏ Identify your preferred style of organizing your life—stacks and piles or neat freak.

❑ Work on making your preferred style work for you rather than changing to a different style.

❑ Plan your family and personal activities into your calendar.

❑ Stop procrastinating.

❑ When you get too many irons in the fire, stop, take a minute to catch your breath, and ask yourself what you can do to survive.

❑ Find somewhere to "dump" your ideas using either a high- or low-tech methods.

Build a Network of Strong Relationships

❑ Work on expanding your network of friends or trusted colleagues at work.

❑ If you have a subordinate who is also a friend, talk with that person to clarify how the two of you are handling both roles.

❑ Look for at least one colleague who will tell you when you're screwing up.

❑ Let people help you more often.

❑ Take some actions to be a good friend to colleagues and don't keep score.

❑ Work on becoming a great listener.

Defending Yourself from Toxic People

❑ Identify toxic people in your life.

❏ Eliminate the toxic people from your life if you can. Limiting contact or confronting them are other options.

❏ Work on surrounding yourself with people who are healthy for you to be around to dilute the impact of toxic people in your life.

❏ If you're a toxic person, admit it and do something about it. Get professional help if necessary.

Be a Good Team Member

❏ Concentrate on the positive aspects of the team's work and focus on how to overcome the obstacles that are in your way.

❏ If you're a team leader, make sure the team members understand the vision and have the training they need to succeed.

❏ Don't take credit for the team's work. Make sure you give credit to other people.

❏ Focus on the team goal, not the personality quirks of team members.

Is Your Work Culture Toxic or Inspiring?

❏ Assess whether or not your work culture has changed recently. It may be more or less toxic than it was in the past.

❏ Determine if there is a mismatch between you and your organization's culture. If so, decide whether it's toxic enough for you to leave.

❑ If you're interviewing for a new job, pay attention to the culture. A great job description probably won't outweigh a toxic culture in the long run.

Are You Being "Held Captive" by Your Organization?

❑ Assess whether or not you're being held captive by your organization.

❑ If you're being held captive, develop a plan and set a time line for getting out.

❑ If you must stay in the job, develop a plan for changing your attitude or behavior so the job is more tolerable.

Are You Working for a Toxic Boss or an Inspiring Leader?

❑ Identify the inspiring leaders that you've encountered in your career.

❑ Look for ways to maintain contact with those leaders and opportunities to work for or with them again in the future.

❑ If you're working for a toxic boss, decide if you're going to wait out the situation in the hope that the person will leave.

❑ If you decide that the toxic boss situation isn't likely to change, develop your own plan to change your job.

❑ If you want to be an inspiring leader, read, watch great leaders, and get feedback from people on your skills.

Bibliography

Allen, David. *Getting Things Done: The Art of Stress-Free Productivity*. New York: Viking, 2001.

Baker, Dan. *What Happy People Know: How the New Science of Happiness Can Change Your Life for the Better*. Emmaus, PA: Rodale, 2003.

Biggs, Richard. *Burn Brightly Without Burning Out: Balancing Your Career with the Rest of Your Life*. Nashville: Thomas Nelson, 2002.

Carlson, Richard. *You Can Be Happy No Matter What: Five Principles Your Therapist Never Told You*. Novato, CA: New World Library, 1997.

Covey, Stephen R. *First Things First*. New York: Fireside, 1994.

Frost, Peter J. *Toxic Emotions at Work: How Compassionate Managers Handle Pain and Conflict*. Boston, MA: Harvard Business School Press, 2003.

Groppel, Jack. *The Corporate Athlete: How to Achieve Maximal Performance in Business and Life*. New York: John Wiley and Sons, 2000.

Horn, Sam. *Take the Bully by the Horns: Stop Unethical, Uncooperative or Unpleasant People from Running and Ruining Your Life*. New York: St. Martin's Press, 2002.

Kouzes, James M., and Barry Z. Posner. *Credibility: How Leaders Gain It, Lose It, and Why People Demand It*. San Francisco: Jossey-Bass, 1993.

Loehr, James, and Tony Schwartz. *The Power of Full Engagement*. New York: The Free Press, 2003.

Reinhold, Barbara Bailey. *Toxic Work: How to Overcome Stress, Overload and Burnout and Revitalize Your Career*. New York: Plume, 1997.

Seligman, Martin E.P. *Authentic Happiness: Using the New Positive Psychology to Realize Your Potential for Lasting Fulfillment*. New York: The Free Press, 2002.

Stoltz, Paul G. *Adversity Quotient: Turning Obstacles into Opportunities*. New York: John Wiley, 1997.

Index

A

AARP, 55, 79, 149
Abilities, understanding,
    108–109
Abusive colleagues, 139–149,
    159. *See also* Boss, toxic;
    Toxic people
Abusive work culture, 156,
    159–161. *See also* Toxic
    organizations
Activities, healthy rituals,
    103–104
Adversity, learning from, 7–8.
    See also Transitions, difficult
Advice
    from colleagues, 127
    and job change, 173–174,
        182
Affirmations, 11, 20
After-action reviews, 188
Altruism
    thought category, 12, 13

and work, 29, 30–31, 33, 34,
    43
Angry critic, toxic type, 133
Associations, 124
Athletic training, 22
Attitudes. *See* Mindset and
    attitude
August, Kelsey, 9–10, 91–92
Autobiographies. *See* Personal
    stories
Aynesworth, Tim, 46–47,
    47–48, 54

B

Backstabbing, 132, 133, 155
Bad mood, changing, 10, 81
Bad news, unexpected, 76–77
Balance
    employee/employer, 85–87
    reward/risk, 53, 54, 57, 58
    work/homelife, 40, 66–67,
        69, 110–112, 185–186

work/relaxation. *See* Pace,
  setting
Barrett, Bonnie, 32, 52, 185–186
Benefits. *See* Health insurance;
  Pensions
Betrayal, 138–139
"Big rocks"
  checklist, 193
  identifying, 38–39, 40
"Bionic" reputation, 65. *See also*
  Superhero reputation.
Birkenholtz, Brad, 117
Birkenholtz, Jennifer, 117
BISYS, 70
Blackberry, 116
Blaming, 173
Blotter calendar, 116
Boot, Sandra, 102
Boredom, 32, 52, 173
Boss, great, drawbacks of, 176
Boss, toxic, 139–40, 159,
  175–176, 180
  and career change, 182–184
  checklist, 189, 198
  learning from, 188
  Theory X assumptions,
    181–182
  and trust, 181
Boston Communications Group,
  127
Brainstorming, 146–147
Brandt, Bridget, 40, 115
Breaks, 99–100, 101. *See also*
  Pace, setting; Self-pity breaks
Breathing, 13, 98–99
Bright people, and burnout, 9
Bureaucracies, 90

Burnout
  avoiding, 5–6
  checklist, 192–198
  optimistic side, 3
  origin of, 9, 107
  pessimistic side, 2–3
Buyouts, 173

C
Calendar
  blotter, 116
  family, 110–111
Calming rituals. *See* Breathing;
  Meditation; Prayer; Yoga
Canadian Tire Corporation, 145
Captivity—Jobs
  checklist, 178
  financial, 170–172
  people traps, 175–176
  and positive outlook, 177
  structural, 172–174
Carlisle, Linda, 114, 115–116
Catastrophizing, 14
Catholic Health East, 186
CEOS, friendships, 124
Challenger space shuttle, 112
Change
  disruptive, 3
  fear of, 174
  as improvement, 184
  preparedness, 55–57, 94
Chatter, 10
Checklists
  anti-burnout, 192–198
  big rocks/little stuff, 193
  boss, toxic/inspiring, 198
  control freak, 195

finding meaning, 193
healthy rituals, 103–104, 195
humor, 194
job captivity, 178, 198
keeping options open,
    56–58, 193–194
leaders, 189, 198
organizational style, 195–196
personal story, 194
strong relationships, 196
teamwork, 197
toxic boss, 189, 196–197
toxic colleague, 142
watching thoughts, 192
work culture, 165, 166–167,
    197–198
Cheney, Dick, 32, 108–109
Choices
    generating options, 45–46
    tough, 37–39
Ciccone, Anne Marie, 177
Clean desk *vs.* stacks & piles,
    105–106
Cliques, 79–80, 130
CNA Insurance Company, 89
Colleagues
    and networking, 129–130
    role of, 121–124
    toxic. *See* Toxic people
Collins, Jim, 30
Colton, Sterling, 42, 96, 186
Comfort level, employee, 158
Commando training, mottoes,
    22
Commitment, 17–19, 30–32
Commitments, multiple,
    110–111, 114

Committees, workplace, 89–90
Communication, training, 150
Complaining, 71, 72. *See also*
    Self-pity break
Complete stop, 114
Complexity, dealing with
    relationships, 110–111
    self-knowledge, 108–110
    technology, 114–117
    time, 112–114
Computers, 115, 117
Confidence, team, 87–88
Confrontation, toxic people,
    137–138
Contextual humor, 79–80
Control freaks, 83–84
    checklist, 195
    overly helpful behavior,
        89–90
    and project milestones,
        85–87
    save-the-world mentality,
        91–92
    taking over, team bogged
        down, 87–88
    trust/delegation, 84–85
Controlling correctors, toxic
    type, 133
Conviction, living with, 32–34
Cooperation, 147, 148
Corporate Athlete, The (Groppel),
    101
Corporate reorganization, 45–46
Creativity, 25
Courage
    living with, 32–34
    thought category, 12, 13

Courtesy, 25
Covey, Stephen R., 37
Credibility (Kouzes/Posner), 185
Credit, sharing, 146–147
Crying, 76, 77, 183
Curiosity
    lifelong learning, 32
    thought category, 12, 13

D
Dalkon Shield Claimants Trust,
    150
Delegation, 84–85
Difficult people. *See* Toxic people
Discipline, mental, 21–23
Downtime. *See* Healthy rituals;
    Pace, setting
Dunn, Matthew, 28, 37, 45–46,
    53

E
Education, and time manage-
    ment, 112–113
e-mail
    checking, 99–100
    sending to oneself, 116
Emotions, and thinking. link.,
    12, 13
Employees
    lack of respect for, 183–184
    retention of, 121, 182
    (toxic) assumptions about,
        181–182
Encouragement, 127
End-running, 90
Energy recovery breaks. *See*
    Breaks
Environmental scanning

checklist, 57
    external, 49–51
    internal, 51–53
Ernst & Young, 62, 111, 164
Ethical standards, 41–43
Exercise
    mental (Covey), 37
    physical, 38–39, 93
Expectations
    mismatch, 158–159
    realistic, 108–109
    reducing, 37–39
    unrealistic, 123
External scanning, 49–51
    checklist, 57
External voice, 52–53
Eyes, smiling with, 81, 82

F
Facial expressions, 81–82
Fairness, trust component, 181
Family
    activities, organizational tool,
        117
    priority, 37, 38, 102,
        110–111
    rituals, 95
    supportive, 121
    work balance, 40, 66–67, 69,
        110–112, 185–186
Family business
    and ethical reputation, 42
    integrating non-family staff,
        161–163
Fannie Mae, 30
Favoritism, 123
Feedback
    from colleague, 128, 188

team leaders, 147
to toxic bosses, 184
First Things First (Covey), 37
Fisher, Margaret, 40, 55, 78, 148–149
Flat organizations, 150
Flexibility
 teamwork, 148–149
 work hours, 185–186
Formal leaders, 179, 185
"42 Long" leadership model, 187
Foster, Len, 145
"Found" time, 112–113
Freedom & options, thought category, 12, 13. *See also* Options.
Freeman, Julie, 37–38, 64, 101, 150
Friendships, maintaining, 38, 39
Friendships—at work, 119–120
 behaviors, 132
 checklist, 196
 downside of, 122–124
 types of help provided by, 127–129
 value of, 121–122
Fripp, Patricia, 83
Future
 obsessing about, 16
 positive thoughts about, 20

G
Gallagher, Ed, 21–22, 81, 126
Gallows humor, 80
Gallup Strengths-Based assessment, 52
Galuszka, Joe, 2, 43, 110

Gandhi, Mahatma, 61
Gardner, Ken, 179
Gatten, Nate, 30, 70
Gemmell, Ginna, 7, 48, 151, 163, 173–174, 183
Giammalvo, Peter, 186–187
Gladwell, Malcolm, 107
Glass ceiling, 172
GlidePath, Inc.. Alexandria, VA., 7, 48, 163, 173
Glover, Barbara, 11, 12, 130
Goals
 life, 47–49, 56–57
 occupational, 177, 178
Golden handcuffs, 170–172
Goodman, Andy, 27–28, 31, 52–53
Good mood, 10, 81
Good to Great (Collins), 30
Goold, Glen, 111, 164
Goold, Linda, 77–78, 110
Gossip, 132
Government jobs, 171
Granese, Nancy, 99
Gratitude, thought category, 12, 13
Gregory, Jamie, 29, 100, 116, 146, 150
Groppel, Jack, 101
Grudges, 132
Guidici, Jim, 70

H
Happiness
 and actions, 81
 and content of thoughts, 12, 13
Hawley, Jack, 26

Index

Health & energy, thought category, 12, 13
Health insurance, 170
Healthy rituals, 93–94
breathing, 98–99
checklist, 103–104, 195
pacing yourself, 100–101
sleep, 97
time off, 99–100
untraditional, 94–97
Healthy work cultures, 161–163
Help
asking for, 131
offering, 131
types of, 127–129
Hero
definition, 61
and personal story, 61–63
Hierarchies, organizational, 172
High achievers. *See* Superhero
reputation
High-tech organizing tools,
114–115
Hill, Steve, 33, 106
Hobbies, 39
Home projects, 39
Honesty, 25. *See also* Trust.
Humor
applied in bad situation,
63–64, 67, 71–75
to blow off steam, 78
checklist, 194
to connect with people/make
point, 74–75
to maintain perspective,
77–78, 122
See also Contextual joke;

Gallows humor; Laughter;
Private joke; Smiling

I
IBM, 179
Ideas, downloading, 116–117
"I Have a Dream" speech (King), 61
Inc. 500 list, 9, 91
Informal leaders, 179, 185
Information, hoarding, 159
Inkley, Lowell, 42
Innovation projects, 151
Inspiring leaders, 180
checklist, 198
defined, 185
positive aspects of, 184–185
and trust, 181
Inspiring organizations, 153,
155, 157
checklist, 165, 197–198
Internal scanning, 51–53
checklist, 57
See also Self-knowledge;
Vision, developing.
Internal voice, 52–53
International Association of
Business Communicators, 37,
64, 101, 150
Interpersonal relations, training,
150
Intrawest (Vancouver), 28, 45, 53
Intuition, job interview, 164

J
Jernigan, Cheryl, 7, 83–84, 123
Jernigan, Jeff, 84–85, 105, 154,
174

Job
  expectations, mismatch,
    158–159
  fit, 174
  government, 171
  interview, 164
  leaving, approach, 177
  love, but toxic boss, 184
  motivation to change, 82–84
  rut, 173–174. *See also*
    Captivity—Jobs
Jokes. *See* Humor; Laughter
Jones, Vickie J., 2, 108

K
Kindness
  and laughter, 78
  thought category, 12, 13
King, Martin Luther, Jr., 61
Knowledge workers, 173, 186
Kouzes, James M., 185
KPMG, 62
Kulbick, Bob, 35–36, 74–75,
  89–90, 125–126
Kundis, Ken, 55

L
La Barge, Norman, 31, 112–113,
  180
Laughter, 71, 122
  and building team spirit,
    79–80
  checklist, 194
  and control freak, 89
    See also Humor; Smiling
Lavin, Ina, 94–95, 127
Leaders
  checklist, 189, 198

as experts, 186–187
  formal, 179, 185
  informal, 179, 195
  inspiring. *See* Inspiring leaders
  learning from, 188
Leaders—teams, 143
  effective, traits, 144, 147,
    150
  ineffective, 147
  role of, 145–146, 150, 151
Leadership. 124, 125–126
  opportunities, 188
  skills, developing, 188
  theories, 187
Learning
  from adversity, 7–8
  lifelong, 32
  from mistakes, 188
  from successes, 188
Lifelong engagement, recipe, 34
Lifelong learning, 32
Limits, setting, 66–67
  and toxic people, 136, 137
Linux Clusters, 106
List making, 105, 107, 112, 115
Listening, 131–132
"Little stuff"
  checklist, 193
  identifying, 39, 40–41
Loehr, Jim, 32
Lott, Trent, 146
Loughmiller, Leslie, 105, 183
Love, thought category, 12, 13
Low-tech organizing tools,
  114–115
Loyalty, 25, 32, 34, 125–126
Lunsford, Jim, 26–27, 31, 56,
  110

M

McEntee, Chris, 95, 128
McGregor, Douglas, 181
Magid, Ramona, 128–129
Managers, 124, 150, 179
Manipulative behavior, 155
Mantras, 11
Marine training, 21
Marriott International, 42, 96, 186
Martial arts training, 21, 22
Mattson, Linda, 125
Meals, family, 95
Meaning
    focus on, 43
    thought category, 12, 13
Meaning, finding, 25
    checklist, 193
    commitment, 30–32
    passion, 26–28
    purpose, 28–30
    spiritual energy, 32–34
Meditation, 13, 93, 98
Meltdown, 114
Memory, 116, 117
Mental habits, managing, 11
Mental lists, 116
Mental toughness, 21–23
Micromanagement, 40, 83–84, 85, 89–90. *See also* Control freaks
Mikesh, Robert, 43
Milestones, project, 85–86, 87
Military training, 17–19, 21–22
Mindset & attitudes, 7–8
    thoughts, 9–23
Mismatch

employee/work culture, 157–159
    job expectations, 158–159
Mission, organization, 30
Mistakes, learning from, 188

N

National Association of Realtors, 28, 100, 116, 146
Neat freak, 105
Network, informal relationships, 129–130
Notebooks, 114–116

O

Optimism
    components of, 13–15
    curve, project cycle, 151
    thought category, 12, 13
Options
    checklist, 56–58, 193–194
    generating, 45–47
Options—building
    building portfolio of options, 53–55
    conducting environmental scanning, 49–53
    cultivating readiness to change, 55–56
    developing vision, 47–49
Organizational behavior, 148, 149. *See also* Leaders
Organizational captivity, 169
    changing attitude to, 177
    types of, 170–176
Organizational structure
    flat, 150

pyramidal hierarchy, 172.
    See also Work culture
Organizing style, 105–117
    checklist, 195–196
Overly helpful behavior, 89–90
Overreacting, 5, 183
Overthinking, 10
Owen, Harrison, 26

P
Pace, setting, 66–67, 100–102
Palm Pilot, 114–116
Park, Craig, 14–15, 50,
    119–120
Passion
    for personal interests, 28
    turning into business, 27–28
    for work, 26–28, 48
Past, focusing on, 6, 16
Pate Moulton, Shana, 29, 48, 76
Patel, Ashwin, 50, 61–62
Patience, 14–15, 138
PDAs. *See* Personal digital assis-
    tants
Peace of mind, 42, 43
Peat Marwick Mitchell, 42
Pensions, 170, 171
Perfectionism, 6, 37–39, 84. *See
    also* Superhero reputation
Permanent *vs.* temporary. opti-
    mism., 14, 15
Perseverance, 32, 34
Personal digital assistants.
    PDAs., 114. *See also* Palm
    Pilot
Personal interests, cultivating,
    28

Personality, company. *See* Work
    culture
Personality conflicts, 148,
    149–150
Personality measures, 52
Personal story, 59, 60
    checklist, 194
    hero or victim, 61–63
    moral of, 64–65
    and superhero reputation,
        65–67
    tone of, 63–64
Perspective
    and colleague feedback, 128
    maintaining, 35–43
Pessimism curve, project cycle,
    151
Pessimists, 14, 133, 134, 136
Place, enjoyment of, 96
Pleasures, simple, 16
Pollak, Jane, 27–28
Positive mental attitude, 10, 11,
    13, 43, 81, 177
Positive psychology, 13–14
Posner, Barry Z., 185
Power of Full Engagement
    (Loehr/Schwartz), 32–33
Power-sharing, teamwork, 148
Prayer, 7, 8, 11, 43, 98. *See also*
    Spirituality
Present, focus on, 16–19
Priorities, setting, 37, 38, 102
    "little stuff," identifying, 39,
        40–41
    and relationships, 37, 38,
        102, 110–111
    and self-knowledge, 108

what you don't want, 46–47
Private joke, 79–80
Proactivity, thought category, 12, 13
Problems, attachment to, 10, 14, 15
Procrastination, 112, 113
Professional associations, 124
Professional workers, 186. *See also* Knowledge workers.
Project cycle, 151
Projects, bogged down, 87–88
Promise-keeping, trust component, 181
Purpose
  thought category, 12, 13
  of work, 28–30
Pyramid hierarchies, 172

Q
Questions, asking, 109

R
Raphaelian, Gene, 34, 55, 119
Rasmussen, Ray, 11, 53, 131, 157
Recovery rituals. *See* Healthy rituals
Reese, Chad, 2, 51–52, 71–72
Relationships
  checklist, 196
  and complexity, 107
  good, 119–120, 121, 131–132
  high-trust, 138–140
  informal, 129–130, 185
  superior/subordinate, 123, 124, 150, 175–176

toxic. *See* Toxic people
  visualizing, 20
  (*See also* Family; Friendships.
Relaxation techniques, 93. *See also* Breathing.
Repititious phrases. *See* Affirmations; Mantras; Prayers
Reporting relationship, 123, 124, 150, 175–176
Reputation
  and ethical standards, 42
  superhero, 65–67
Respect, trust component, 181, 183–184
Responsibilities
  multiple, 110–111, 114
  tracking, 113
Resumes, 55, 57
Retirement benefits, 170, 171
Reviews, after-action, 188
Risk/reward
  balance, 53, 54, 57
  and leaving job, 171, 172
Rostenkowski, Dan, 144–145
RSKCo, 89
Ruts, 173–174. *See also* Captivity – Jobs.

S
Salary, 170
Save-the-world mentality, 91–92
Saying "no," 41–42, 136
Scanning. *See* Environmental scanning
Schwartz, Tony, 32
Sebree, John, 28–29, 146–147, 151

Self-talk, 10
Self-confidence, 14
Self-knowledge, 107–110. *See also* Internal scanning; Vision, developing.
Self-pity breaks, 75–77
Seligman, Martin E. P., 13–14
Sexual harassment, 160–161
Shaffer, Chelsea, 22–23, 86
Skills
    internal scanning, 51–53
    leadership, 188
    learning new, 55. *See also* Lifelong learning.
Sleep, 97
Smiling, 81–82
Smith, Al, 179
Social Security Administration (U.S.), 115
Social Life of Paper, The (Gladwell), 107
Soul Proprietor (Pollak), 27
Spiral-ring notebooks, 114–116
Spiritual energy, 32–34
Spirituality
    thought category, 12
    and work, 25
Stacks and piles *vs.* clean desk, 105–106, 107
Standards, ethical, 41–43
Storytelling, 59–60
    funny, 72–73, 80
    and hero prototype, 61
    as teaching tool, 64–65
    (*See also* Personal story.
Strengths, maximizing, 108, 113
Success
    elements of, 3

learning from, 188
secrets of, 4
visualizing, 20, 22
Suchanick, Mike, 21
Superhero reputation, 65–67
Supervisors, 123, 124, 179
Support group, 125–125
Swearingen, Alice, 22, 29, 78, 94

T

Tasks, help with, 127, 128–129
Team confidence, 87–88
Team members—traits
    cooperate/share credit, 146–147
    get along with everyone, 148–151
    make boss/org. look good, 144–146
Team spirit, and laughter, 79–80
Teamwork, 25, 125–126, 143
    checklist, 197
Technology, and organizational habits, 107
Television, 93
Templates, electronic, 117
Theory X assumptions, 181–182
Thiokol (aerospace), 112
Thoughts, 9–23
    categories, 12–13
    choosing, 12
    content of, 12
    and happiness, 12, 13
    managing, 10–11
    watching, checklist, 192
Time management, 107, 112–113, 153. *See also*

Multiple responsibilities.
To-do list, 105, 112, 115, 116
Tone, personal story, 63
Toughness training, 21–23
Toxic boss. *See* Boss, toxic
Toxic organizations, 153, 154,
    157
    assessing, 163–164
    causes, 156
    checklist, 166–167, 197–198
        See also Work culture
Toxic people
    checklist, 142, 196–197
    confronting, 137–138
    cultivating high-trust
        relationships, 138–140
    eliminating, 134–135
    limiting contact with,
        135–137
    self test, 140–141
    types of, 120
Transitions, difficult, 108–109
    and friendships, 120, 123,
        125–126, 130
Trust
    components of, 181
    and delegation, 84–85
    and ethical standards, 42
    and inspiring leaders, 181
    and relationships at work,
        120, 121, 122, 126,
        138–140
    and teamwork, 147
    and toxic bosses, 181,
        183–184
Truth-telling, trust component,
    181
Turner, Amy, 32, 40, 149, 176

U
Understanding, 78
Unexpected bad news, 76–77
Union Bank (Kansas City), 84,
    154
Universal *vs.* specific view (opti-
    mism), 14
Unproductive work culture,
    159–161
Untraditional healthy rituals,
    94–97
Unwinding. *See* Healthy rituals
U.S. Army, 188
U.S. Congress, 144
U.S. House of Representatives,
    109, 115, 145, 148

V
Vacation, scheduling, 69, 70
Values, incorporating at work,
    25, 32–34
Victim mentality, 59, 61–63,
    169, 173
Victories, celebrating, 96
Vinkenes, Pat, 31, 115, 116, 171
Vision
    checklist, 56–57
    developing, 47–49
Visualization, 20, 22, 98
Volunteerism, 94–95, 188
Volunteers, toxic, 134–135

W
Waters, Averil, 56, 65–66
Wayne Brothers, Inc. (Davidson,
    N.C.), 26, 31, 56, 110
Weaknesses, lessening impact of,
    108, 113

Weekends, 100, 102
Whining, 71, 75, 133
White & Case (law firm), 114
Wismer, Janice, 31
Women in workforce, 172
Women's movement, 172
Woodbury, Rick, 42–43,
    161–163
Work
    commitment to, 30–32
    and friendships at, 119–124
    homelife, 40, 66–67, 69,
        110–111, 185–186
    and inner life, 27–28
    passion for, 26–28
    purpose, 28–30
    and spiritual energy, 32–34

time off, 69, 70, 99–100
transitions, 108–109
Work culture, 30, 153, 155
    abusive, 159–161
    assessing, 163–164
    checklist, 197–198
    defined, 156–57
    healthy, 161–163
    mismatches, 157–159
Worst-case planning, 50

Y
Yoga, 98

Z
Zaleznik, Abraham, 148